# Manager's Guide to Cost Reduction

Written and Illustrated by Janice Czaplewski
© Copyright 2013
All rights reserved

## Preface

In this economy, if ever there was a time to use a howitzer to attack the castle where the profits are stored, this is it. Well, maybe it's not quite that serious, but you certainly can't sit back and just hope it gets better. The only way it will get better is if you are proactive, and the sooner you start the more impact you can have.

Just remember that if you always do what you always did, you will always get what you always got.

This book will help you evaluate your situation to see if you need to do a cost reduction project, help you choose the project, walk you through the steps of a project, and even take it to the next level with cost containment. After you have done the work to reduce the costs, you want to make sure they don't creep up on you.

There are some really good tips to make the process easier and at the end of the book there are even "Excel Hints" to help you with the spreadsheets. As anyone who has worked with Excel knows, there is more than one way to perform functions. Some people prefer drop down boxes and some prefer to right click. I will show you only one way, but you can figure out others after you get familiar with the objectives.

This book is for managers to get an overview of the process. Order our full color companion workbook for your employees to use as a blueprint for your projects.

> *If you would like to share your success stories or if you would like help with your Cost Reduction Projects or Cost Containment Projects, fell free to contact us. We can help you assess your need for a project, choose your projects, set them up, or even train your people to do it internally using our proven methods – whatever suits your needs.*
>
> *Janice@entire360.com*

## *Chapters*

1. *Introduction* .......................... 5
2. *Seven Truths about Manufacturing Cost*............................................ 12
3. *Why Spend the Time and Money* ... 16
4. *Cost Reduction Verses Cost Containment* ................................ 27
5. *Evaluation Questions – Do You Need to Do A Project?* ....................... 34
6. *Getting Started*.......................... 44
7. *How to Choose Your Target*...........52
8. *Set Up* ...................................... 58
9. *Evaluation* ............................... 67
10. *Quoting* ................................... 74
11. *Summary Evaluation* ..................100
12. *Cost Containment*..................... 113
13. *Cost Containment Analysis* ......... 130
14. *Summary* ................................. 148
15. *Excel Hints* .............................. 157

## *Chapter 1 – Introduction*

Are you tired of fighting the same old battle of rising manufacturing / material costs? You are not alone. Every company is fighting the same battle. But if you are using a catapult and your competition is using a 155 Howitzer, you may find yourself out gunned.

What do they know that you don't know? They know that for every $1.00 you spend on cost reduction, you can *save* $4.00 to $10.00 dollars – or more. That's money that goes directly to your bottom line. After all, you have already paid all your overhead. Whether you make $100.00 on a part or $1000.00 on a part, the building, utilities, labor, insurance, etc. still cost the same.

Every year material costs rise, labor costs rise, utility costs rise, insurance costs rise and taxes rise. What is the only thing not rising? Your profits!

Whether you own the company, are in charge of the whole company, are in charge of a department, or do the purchasing for the company, you must always be trying to reduce costs. It's not only part of your job; it's the smart thing to do because a healthy company is a stable company.

People that waste money because it's "not their money" are always the ones that are surprised when the company downsizes. Whether you like your job or not, you probably like being employed or at the very least you like getting a paycheck, so you need to do everything you can to help make sure the company stays around.

The first year I was a buyer, we had four suppliers close their doors in the first three months of the year. Many other companies were laying people off or pounding the pavement looking for more business so they didn't have to downsize. Some of these companies had been in business a long time and it was a little scary. If these long term companies went out of business, what might happen to ours?

When I was working as a maintenance supervisor, I worked on 43$^{rd}$ and Lincoln in Milwaukee, Wisconsin. That area had been filled with manufacturing plants for 75 years. Now, the company I worked for is one of the very few remaining businesses in the area.

One day a maintenance employee was complaining about the fact that the company was bringing in some outside contractors to do some work. He said, "Maybe we should go on a work slow-down to protest them taking our jobs away." I told him that the best way to _keep_ his job was to _do_ his job and that if he was in any doubt about that being a real threat; he only needed to look outside and see all the empty buildings that surrounded the plant. Some of those companies were bigger than ours, had been around longer than ours and were names that the general public would recognize – unlike ours. After he thought about it awhile, he said "I never thought about it that way before." All he could see was the immediate threat that was right before his eyes and not the bigger threat that was lurking around the corner.

Whether you are talking about a work slow-down or not doing everything you can to reduce costs, you are running the risk of helping yourself become unemployed. Even a company that is healthy has to do everything it can to increase profits. After all, there are owners or shareholders that are expecting to make money. Just making a wild guess here, but I think making money is probably pretty high on the list of reasons they are involved in the company in the first place. If they no longer make money or no longer make as _much_ money as they want, they may decide to rethink their decision. That could cause the company to downsize, be sold to someone else or close entirely. Where would that leave you?

While cost reduction projects are not for the faint of heart, they are not overwhelming for anyone with better-than-basic computer skills, attention to detail, and some common sense. The only other thing you need is a blueprint for doing the projects. This book can serve as your blueprint.

What about resistance to doing the projects? Make no mistake: there _will_ be some resistance. People tend to avoid doing anything that will change the status quo. That's just human nature. How many times have you heard someone say, "That's the way we have always done it."? Every time I hear that I want to explain that, "Yes, and we used to live in caves and huddle around a fire and hunt with spears, but we have gotten smarter than that!" Just because we "always did it that way" does not mean it is still the only way to do it or <u>even the best way</u>.

Upper management may resist because they don't see the value, don't want to make changes, haven't realized the need or are too busy with more urgent issues.

Buyers may resist because they don't want the extra work or don't want to learn a complicated new process or because they think they are already doing a great job. Even if they _are_ doing a great job, there is still more they could be doing.

Not only are we out of the caves we once lived in, we have more tools available than ever before to view, locate, evaluate, manipulate, transmit, store, and share information. Just as the 155 Howitzer has replaced the catapult, we must replace our old way of doing business and make use of the available technology or be left behind.

This is the time to introduce "New Corporate Math" to your workplace. With "Old Corporate Math", if you want to <u>add</u> to the bottom line, you <u>subtract</u> employees and <u>divide</u> the work. With the "New Corporate Math" you can simply <u>multiply</u> your results by <u>adding</u> a proven process and working smarter.

As you go through the chapters of this book, you will learn the difference between a cost reduction project and a cost containment project and how to decide if you need to do one or the other – or both and which is best for you. It will help you choose the best target and resources for your project. These are areas where management will have the most involvement.

After these decisions are made, you will be shown how to set up a project, how to evaluate it, how to run it and how to create the summary. The layouts and formulas are included in order to make it easier.

In addition to cost savings, you will see shortened lead times, longer quote expiration dates, less mistakes in purchase order delivery dates, quantities and data entry. You will be able to track increases by commodity, supplier or buyer. You will even be able to pinpoint areas that need attention.

OEM's always seem to be caught in the middle between the suppliers and the customers. Your suppliers continue to raise their prices but your customers expect you to hold yours. With this proven process you can hold your pricing to your customers without decreasing your profit margin.

There's no black magic involved, or even any white magic, for that matter. You just have to apply the proven methods shown in this book.

This book is intended for management as well as the people doing the projects. If you aren't sure if you need to do a project, this book will help you to decide. If you have never done a large cost reduction or cost containment project before, you can use this as your handbook.

Note that I have tried to leave enough room in the margins for any notes you may wish to make while reading this book.

If you are wondering if this is worth the time and cost, I can tell you it is. I can't *guarantee* you will save money, but I can tell you one thing for certain – <u>*every Cost Reduction project we have ever done has saved much more than it cost.*</u>

## *Chapter 2 – Seven Truths about Manufacturing Costs*

Whether you manufacture millions of little parts or a dozen huge machines, these seven truths always apply.

1. *Materials make up the largest portion of manufacturing costs*
2. *Costs of materials go up every year*
3. *Every cost increase has to be funded by your possible profits*
4. *Eighty percent of your material increases are on twenty percent of your parts*
5. *Most buyers try hard to contain costs but are too overworked to be proactive*
6. *It is not always possible or advisable to pass cost increases along to your customers*
7. *If you want to increase profit, you have to decrease material costs*

Many manufactures will tell you that material costs are 60% to 80% of their entire manufacturing costs. With this being the most expensive part of your business, and one of the few you can control, doesn't it make sense to put the majority of your efforts here?

Every year your suppliers increase their prices because their suppliers are increasing the prices to them. If every link in the chain passes along those increases, your product may become too expensive for your customers to buy. Either that or you hold your pricing and watch your profit margin dwindle. Neither of those choices is good, especially when there are other choices available.

As your prices increase, your profits decrease because you sell less units. Holding or reducing prices will increase your profits.

Some materials seem to stay the same price for long periods of time. Some are more reactive to the cost of steel, gas, foreign markets, etc. If you have 100,000 part numbers in your inventory, perhaps 30% of those cost less than $2.00. Maybe another 50% of those are more expensive but still not the "heavy hitters". That last 20% is where you spend the majority of your money. Look at it like your household budget. Every month you write checks totaling $5000.00 to ten different places. The two largest checks may be for your house and your car. If your house costs $3000.00 and your car is $1000.00, you have spent 80% of your monthly budget on those two things. Yet they are only 20% of the checks you write.

Most buyers understand the principal and really do try to hold costs. Unfortunately, they probably wear many hats, especially in this economy. They are so busy with day to day tasks that they simply don't have the time to worry about every price increase.

Your profits are the reason you are in business. If your profits are smaller either because you absorbed the increases or you lost business because you increased your pricing, your own _personal_ purchasing power is affected. The sad news is that while your purchasing power is going down because of this, you are losing even more purchasing power because your gas, groceries, clothing, vacations, etc. are getting more expensive. At some point your standard of living will suffer.

If you want to increase profit, you have to decrease costs. That is the only thing that will keep you competitive in the world market. Your fixed costs are going to either remain the same or, more likely, increase. You could try cutting wages or cutting bonuses, but that is a demon you don't want to unleash unless you really have to. Loyalty will go right out the window – and so will your productivity. Your best employees will start looking for other jobs and they <u>will</u> find them. Your average employees will decide they really don't care enough to give their very best. Your less-than-average employees will stay out of sight and continue to plod along under the radar. They really never do leave, do they?

These truths are things we all know and understand, but sometimes we get so caught up in putting out the daily fires in our jobs that we forget to think about them.

## *Chapter 3 – Why spend the time and money?*

There are many reasons it makes sense to do a cost reduction project or a cost containment project or both. Here are a few.

### **Saving Money**

Being proactive with cost reduction will initially cost some money. There is no getting around that. It will also *save* your company money. That is a given. That is also the biggest reason for doing a project.

### **Free up Time for Buyers**

By using this method, you actually free up time for your buyers to tend to other issues because they will be doing less requoting, issuing and tracking fewer purchase orders and making fewer corrections to purchase orders. They will also know that the prices they have in the system are accurate, so there will be less time spent verifying prices when they need to issue a purchase order.

### Easiest Way to Make Money

Money saved on a cost reduction project is the *easiest* way to add to your bottom line. It doesn't require adding a new production line, hiring more people, or expanding your building. Since it can be started almost immediately it can give you real savings within two to three months.

### Avoid Increasing Your Prices

While increasing your pricing to your customers is an option, it is not necessarily the best option – or even a good one. Companies get price increases all the time. Our customers don't like it any better than we do. As a buyer, every time we got a price increase, I would think, "Isn't this company smart enough to negotiate better pricing?" Okay, so that's not a <u>fair</u> thought, but it is an <u>honest</u> one. Do you want your customers thinking that about you?

### Better Corporate Image

If every one else is raising their pricing and you are holding or even decreasing your pricing slightly, your company will be perceived as being very business savvy. Who doesn't want that kind of image?

## **Company is More Competitive**

If your company makes an automated bar-b-queue grill with a freezer in it that can thaw and season your steak, put it on the grill, turn it, cook it to exactly medium rare, and bring it to the table, you are probably the only company in the world that makes one and you can set your price where you want. For all the rest of us, there is competition. If you raise your prices and your competitors don't, you may lose business.

## **Inventory Costs Money**

As you run a cost reduction project, one of the many things you will evaluate is how many of each piece to buy. By being smarter about the quantities and negotiating with the suppliers, you can reduce the quantity of parts you have to keep on your shelf. By basing your purchases on *realistic* quantities, this also saves money and increases inventory turns.

## **Price Increases Cost Money**

I'm not just talking about the direct cost increase. If you accept the increase without quoting or negotiating, it costs money. If you requote every time there is an increase, it costs time. Like most companies, do you only requote when there is a cost increase? If that is so, you are losing the opportunity to reduce some costs.

## **Extend Quote Expiration Dates**

Most suppliers are looking ahead for future business and, like the rest of us, they like things that are easy. If you are doing a cost reduction project based on future business (maybe for the next quarter), the suppliers are usually willing to extend their quote expiration dates. We have gone from one to two week quote expiration dates to six to nine months. In some cases suppliers are even holding them for an entire year or more. This saves your company and the supplier time requoting. If you have common parts (parts that are used in several places or on several different machines) you may be buying the parts on a regular basis. If that is the case, your buyers don't have to verify pricing each time; they already know the price is still good and that it is the best price.

## **Bundling**

A cost reduction project gives you the opportunity to bundle similar parts. If you have a left and a right hand part and you buy 10 of each, you get one price. If you buy 10 of each <u>at the same time</u>, you can get pricing equivalent to 20 pieces. Usually parts are only ordered when the demand hits the system. Those two parts may not hit the system at the same time, so they are not "visible" to the buyer. This means they are usually bought separately – at the higher cost.

Everyone knows that large companies have better buying power. But what if you are a small or mid sized company? What do you do? If you are a small company, <u>*act*</u> like a big company. Pull together similar parts and see if you can get better pricing on the package. It gives the supplier more incentive, helps them to plan better and gives you better pricing.

NOTE: It is always a good idea to bundle mating parts. If they come up for purchase at different times, they may go to different suppliers. If they don't fit properly when you get them in house, which supplier do you call?

How can they not fit if they are both in spec? Maybe it is a machined part with a tolerance of +/- .03 inches. If both parts are made to the + .03 inch dimension, that is .12 inches more than if they are both made to the - .03 inch dimension. That is a <u>big</u> difference.

Are you wondering how mating parts could come up for purchase at different times? Don't you usually use them together? Maybe an extra one was purchased at some point for R&D or a customer sample or repair. Maybe one was scrapped and it threw the purchasing cycle off. Maybe when the part was originally set up there were different values put in for the EBQ. It doesn't really matter why it happened; it just needs to be corrected.

## **Take Advantage of a Weak Economy**

During a weak economy, suppliers are desperately looking for work. They will be more than happy to quote work at lower prices and with longer quote expiration dates if they know it will result in steady work. If you aren't requoting you are missing a real opportunity to get better pricing while the suppliers are "hungry".

## **Only Reason NOT to do a Cost Reduction Project**

You are already making more money that you know what to do with. If that is the case, then you don't need to do a cost reduction project. You don't need to work, either, so why aren't you retired?

There is more than one way to do a cost reduction. You can do it internally using people that have some free time. You can do it externally with a consultant. You can combine the two.

Finding someone internally that has spare time may not be easy. Most people have more than enough work to fill their day. If they do have an extra 300 hours to spend on a project, it has to make you wonder what they have been doing with all that spare time. Why weren't they asking for more work already? If it's because they aren't that ambitious, maybe they aren't the person you want on the project in the first place.

An outside consultant is a good choice if you can find one who understands the concepts and you feel will be dedicated to saving you as much money as possible. They need to be willing to learn your system so they can use it like an insider would. They have to be trustworthy. After all, you will be giving them access to your drawings and pricing information. You want someone you believe will do a "stellar" job for you, not just an "adequate" job. If they have references it would help.

You could have an external consultant set up the spreadsheets and formulas and then evaluate the information to determine quantities to quote. They would then hand the spreadsheet over to your internal people to do the actual quoting and fill in the spreadsheet. After the quotes are in, the consultant can take the project back, evaluate it and create the summary sheet with formulas to pull in the information required. If you have several buyers, you could split the project among them so it can be completed sooner. They just need to all share the same worksheet.

A better solution would be to choose the best person and then spread some of their other work to other people leaving only one person in charge of the project. Otherwise, when an error occurs, you will find "Nobody" changed that cell. Good luck finding "Nobody." He is an elusive creature.

Generally, buyers are really good at buying. That's not surprising. After all, it's what they were hired for. However, they are not necessarily good at cost reductions. Sure, they can requote a part when needed, but what about an entire project?

People think if they can run a report that gives them a spreadsheet and add a column with a predetermined simple formula to copy (like =E3*G3) they are good at Excel. However, when there are a couple dozen formulas (some very complex) and 100,000 cells to manage, it tends to spiral out of control very quickly. Even if you tell them not to change any formulas or change the columns, I can guarantee they will. Because they really do _want_ to do a good job, at some point they will want to see how they are doing compared to the target and they will plug in numbers and overwrite formulas.

Even the best "Excel guru" can mess up a spreadsheet of this size. The real talent is in being able to find the errors and correct them. On some projects, it takes longer to fix the errors than it did to set up the formulas in the first place. Sorting is also a skill that people do well at on a small spreadsheet, but tend to have a harder time with on large spreadsheets.

We had set up an Excel spreadsheet test for screening applicants for a company when they were hiring a buyer. It was a pretty simple test that checked to see if they could create a simple formula, copy and paste, sort, add, etc. Surprisingly, only one in ten could pass it. This was after they had assured us they were "very good" with Excel.

## *Chapter 4 - Cost Reduction Verses Cost Containment*

Cost Reduction and Cost Containment are both very good tools and are designed to save money. The basic difference is in how you go about them. What you are willing to put into them will determine what you get out of them.

Cost Reduction is aimed at <u>reducing</u> the cost on every part possible within the project. The machine or production line is broken down into individual pieces, evaluated and requoted.

But what happens after the project? Costs tend to creep up again. The quote expires and the new price is higher. The buyers don't bother to requote when there are small increases. Soon you find that you are again spending more than you need to on materials.

Cost Containment is a way of <u>holding</u> costs by tracking all purchases relative to the established price. If there is an increase it will show up on the spreadsheet and has to have an explanation of what was done to hold, or even reduce, the cost.

Reducing costs is necessary and is a good first step. Since parts get purchased repeatedly, it is important to get the same pricing on subsequent buys. Cost Containment is the logical second step to being proactive with cost reductions. There will be more about Cost Containment later.

If you only have the resources to do one or the other, which should you do? That depends on your circumstances.

Cost Reductions take more time to do and require a higher skill level to accomplish, but have a higher return. Depending on the project you choose, you could see savings of $30,000.00 to $100,000.00 or more on a project. Those are just the savings on that specific project and are fairly visible.

If you have a part on which you saved $5.00 and you need 10 of these parts in order to satisfy the requirements of this project, you have now saved $50.00. Or have you saved more than that? If you buy 100 of these parts a year, you are saving $500.00 for the year. In your project, the $50.00 will be recorded and be visible. The actual savings of $500.00 will not be recorded on the project and, therefore, will not be quite as visible – but it will be just as real. In this way, the savings become exponential. If your project shows you saved $30,000.00, in reality, you may have saved $100,000.00 and just because it doesn't show up on the project, doesn't mean it doesn't reflect on the bottom line.

Additionally, if you are able to get suppliers to hold pricing for 18 months, you will get those savings for even longer.

As we were negotiating for longer quote expiration dates, we explained to one supplier that we were getting that length of time from another supplier. He said that if another company was willing to hold their pricing that long they were probably ripping us off to begin with. I explained to him that some of those were parts that he himself had quoted and come in higher on at one point so I didn't feel the other company was "ripping us off". No, I didn't offer him any cheese with his whine.

Cost Reduction projects are also self sustaining. If you pay the money for the first project, it will pay for itself and pay for the next one, which will pay for itself and pay for the next one. See where I'm going with this? In addition to paying for itself and the next project, you will have all the savings from each project. You may find that you have been overpaying for parts for two years, but since there wasn't a price increase, it wasn't challenged.

Cost Containment takes less time and does not require any more than basic computer and logic skills but has smaller rewards. If you have a program that can run a report capturing the necessary information, it is just a matter of having someone run the report, set up some formulas and evaluate any parts that fall outside of the parameters you set.

The secondary advantage of Cost Containment is that it requires requoting parts that were not on a project. As part of the process, any price increase has to have an explanation about what was done to hold or reduce the cost. This sometimes is simple negotiating, but sometimes it requires requoting the part to other suppliers.

By requoting you may get this part for less money than before. Let's face it, even the most diligent buyer doesn't have time to requote every part they purchase – nor should they. There is a "point of diminishing returns" to consider. Eventually, almost every part you purchase will have a price increase and get requoted anyway. Additionally, requoting every part would overwhelm your buyers *and* your suppliers. Remember, you are only one of many companies your suppliers are dealing with. Just because you spend a million dollars a year with a supplier doesn't mean that someone else doesn't spend a million dollars a <u>month</u>. If you are the small fish in the big pond, they will not be able to give you the high level of attention required for constantly requoting parts.

One time I had a handful of parts that needed to be ordered. Although the original supplier hadn't raised his pricing, I decided to requote the parts. When I finally issued the purchase order, it was at a savings of $17,000.00 over the original pricing. And that was only <u>one</u> purchase order. It does pay to look multiple places for savings.

With inflation at 3%, you would expect your material costs to increase 2-3% per year. So if you were able to hold your total increase to less than 1%, would you be thrilled? Probably. But you can do even better. Between the Cost Reduction and the Cost Containment, you could actually see a <u>decrease</u> in your overall material costs. How competitive would that make your company? How happy would that make your owner or shareholders or board of directors? How happy would they be with you? You'd be their shining star!

Another benefit of a Cost Containment project is that you can sort your quarterly results by several different categories. You can identify which suppliers have more increases – or larger dollar increases. You can identify which commodities have more increases – or larger dollar increases. You can even identify if one buyer allows more cost increases than the others. This will help pinpoint areas to look at for improvements.

In case you haven't guessed it yet, neither one of these actually <u>cost</u> you money because of the payback, so why not do both? Even if you paid a person full time to do these two things and nothing else, they would probably be the only person in the company that paid for themselves – and more. Expecting an ROI of 200% to 300% (or even more) on a cost reduction project is not unrealistic. In fact, it's what you *should expect*.

Just to put it in perspective, if all the money we saved one company last year had been given to the employees as bonuses, *every person in the company* would have received around $9,400.00. Not a bad motivator for employees – or owners either for that matter.

## *Chapter 5 - Evaluation Questions – Do You Need To Do A Project?*

Basically, you need to know what's working and what's not working. That's not as easy as it sounds because we don't tend to be proactive in all the areas we should. The old saying "You may not like what's on the TV, but you watch it because it's too much work to get up and change the channel" is a good example. Well, it would be if you are over 50 and remember television before remote controls were invented.

Okay, how about the 51/49 rule? As long as something is 51% good and only 49% bad, we tend to put up with it. It may not be ideal, but it isn't worth the effort to change it. Think of an employee that is "merely adequate". He or she generally gets the job done, but doesn't really do a "stellar" job. Do you fire them? Generally you keep them because they don't draw attention to themselves. Although they will never be 100% good or even 80% good; they are still 51% good. Now if they start coming in late every day or start paying less attention to detail and make mistakes, they get the bosses attention in a negative way. That may tip the scales to the point of only being 49% good. Now they come under scrutiny.

Another reason to keep a person that is "merely adequate" is that they have been there a long time. The general assumption is that because of their longevity, they know everything they need to know and, therefore, are good at their job. They may not have learned anything new in 20 years but they are considered "smart". Look at the desk you are sitting at as you read this. Has is been there a long time? Does that make it smart?

The funny thing about that logic is that when a company is hiring a new person, they tend to prefer someone that has worked in the same place for 20 years. They don't want someone that has had several jobs. Tell me though, which one of those people has had to learn new skills in the last 20 years and has proven they are willing <u>and</u> able to learn. Maybe the only reason they stayed 20 years is that they have been exercising their own 51/49 rule and their job was "good enough". Or maybe they were just too lazy to try to improve their situation by looking for a new job. Then the economy got bad and they got laid off. Now they want _you_ to hire them.

Don't get me wrong, there are a lot of good people that stay with a company for a long time. The way to tell the difference is if they are still actively looking for ways to improve themselves and the company. If Clinton was president the last time they came up with a new idea on their own (without being asked) they are probably just staying there out of habit. Remember, the chains of habit are too weak to be felt until they are too strong to be broken.

Here we are back to the excuse "We have always done it that way." Changing the way things are being done is difficult, but it can be done – _once you identify that it needs to be done._

Are you struggling to decide if you need to do a Cost Reduction Project or a Cost Containment Project or maybe both? Do you think maybe your company isn't a good candidate?

This questionnaire will help you identify if there is a need in your company for a Cost Reduction Project or a Cost Containment Project – or both. Is it worth ten minutes to find out if you can save hundreds of thousands of dollars? We think so.

## Questionnaire

1. What type of product do you make?

2. How many individual machines, parts or units do you make per year?

3. How many <u>types</u> of machines, parts or units do you make per year? (SKU's)

4. How many individual pieces make up your finished product?

5. Is the average selling cost of your product over $500.00?

6. What is your total material spend per year?

7. What type of ERP system do you have?

8. Do buyers use the notes section of your MRP system?

9. Do your buyers accept price increases or do they requote every one?

10. Do the buyers regularly requote parts other than if there is a price increase?

11. Are purchase orders reviewed daily for cost increases?

12. Are quarterly reviews conducted to identify areas of largest cost increases?

13. What commodities / suppliers / buyers have the most or highest cost increases?

14. How many buyers do you have?

15. How many purchase orders are written per month?

16. How many line items are there per purchase order (on average)?

17. Are your inventory turns where you want them?

18. What kinds of reports are you able to generate?

**"Reading" the results**

Questions 1 through 5 - If your product is high cost, low volume (but made up of over 200 parts) and it sells for more than $500.00, you are a prime candidate for both a cost reduction project and a cost containment project.

If your product is high volume, low cost, you may only want to do a cost containment project.

Question 6 - If your total "spend amount" for the year is over $4,000,000.00 you are still a good candidate for doing both projects. You will just select your target differently for a high volume versus a low volume manufacturer. See more about that in Chapter 7 – How to Choose Your Target.

Questions 7 and 8 - If you are making full use of your ERP system's notes, you have a very good start. If not, that would be a good first step, even if you never go any further. The notes will help save time for the buyers by having information readily available that they can use every day, such as lead time verified, price, expiration date, when the last price increase occurred, and when the last requote occurred. You may very well still benefit from both the Cost Reduction projects and the Cost Containment projects depending on your answers to the next questions.

Questions 9 and 10 - If requoting only happens at price increases or maybe not even then, you definitely need to do both a cost reduction project and a cost containment project. Your material costs are rising unchallenged. You need to get that under control as quickly as possible.

Questions 11 through 13 - If you do standard reviews on individual parts on a regular basis, you probably don't need to do the cost containment project, only the cost reduction project. If your only review is when accounting is telling you that the price went up on a machine or product line, and you have no idea why, you definitely need to do the cost containment project. This will even help you figure out where to look for the problem.

Questions 14 through 16 – If your buyers are each averaging more than 50 line items per day, they probably have their plate full with purchase orders, acknowledgements, filing, reports, expediting parts and all the other daily tasks. That means that they probably haven't had the time to monitor price increases in any detail. Doing cost reduction projects will help reduce the amount of parts that need to be quoted on a daily basis, freeing buyers up to spend their time on other things. Doing a cost containment project will help monitor the price increases and get your buyers focused on saving costs.

Questions 17 – If you are looking at reducing your inventory turns, the cost reduction project will help you. You will identify the highest quantity you can buy (getting the best price) without having extra parts on the shelf and the lowest quantity you can buy without running out. The secret is to find the quantity that is the balance between too much and not enough.

Question 18 – If you have reports that can pull information for an entire machine or production line, you have the basic capabilities. You can then have other reports written that can pull the parts required per machine as well as purchasing history such as price, supplier, last cost changes, Economic Batch Quantity, and buyer.

## *Chapter 6 - Getting Started*

Now that you have decided you need to do a Cost Reduction Project, how do you get started? Wait a minute. How do I know you are at least considering doing a project? You're still reading, aren't you?

These are the things you will need.

### **Rules**

You will do better if you have a procedure for how to set up a Cost Reduction Project so nothing is missed and all projects are done the same way. You can use this book for your initial procedure and then customize it later to add information that is specific to your company or ERP system.

You will need rules for _how_ to quote. You want to ask for quote expiration date and lead time with every quote. Not all suppliers will give that to you on the first round. In that case, you need to go back to the suppliers and ask for it. It is a lot of extra work, but it is very valuable information to have.

You will need rules on _what_ to quote. Generally any part that costs less than

$2.00 is not worth spending the time to quote. With one exception, all other parts should be requoted. If it was just requoted and there are not any more places to quote, then it should be marked as such and not requoted. That doesn't mean you can't negotiate with the supplier, however. If it was recently requoted but there _are_ more possible places to quote, then it should still be requoted.

**<u>Information</u>**

You will need to choose a target project. How to choose a project will be covered later in this book, but whatever the project, you need to gather information.

You will need the Bill Of Materials broken down into every individual part. This can be done by taking the upper level drawing and physically looking at every part and sub assembly and sub-sub assembly in it and creating a list. Most companies can at least run a report that will create this list along with how many of each part is needed on the machine.

The easiest way, however, is if you can get a report created that will pull in current supplier, current pricing, quantity on hand, and other information for you. That information will be covered later.

## **Personnel**

If you give the project to someone just because, well - they are cheap and they are available, you may find yourself sitting in your boss's office explaining that the spreadsheets were wrong and all those machines they sold are not going to make as much money for the company as he thought. In fact, they will barely break even. Thanks, but no thanks. Not how I want to spend my morning.

If you have someone working on the project that is "merely adequate", don't expect "stellar" results. So what skills are needed?

You will need someone that understands the principals of purchasing. I have seen everything from the "buy it all" mentality to the "One a Day" mentality. With the first one they would buy 5 years worth of things just to keep from having to issue future purchase orders. With the second one, they would buy one 5 cent screw today and then another one tomorrow if it showed up again. There would be four or five open purchase orders for a single part. Then they complained that they had too much work to do. They didn't understand that if they bought a few more at one time, they wouldn't be issuing and tracking as many purchase orders and they would be less busy. There has to be a happy medium that is carefully evaluated on a part by part basis, but there should never be more than two open purchase orders for any one part. If there are, review the EBQ and annual usage first. If the part needs to be ordered, try adding it to an existing purchase order.

Remember that every part that is ordered has to be tracked, received, and put away. It is less work to put away one batch of 12 parts than three batches of four parts each on three separate purchase orders, especially if they arrive in separate packaging or on separate days.

I have seen parts with an economic batch quantity of 1000 and even 2500 when the company uses less than 100 per year!

You will need someone with above average computer skills. They will be sorting and resorting, hiding and unhiding, quoting and requoting and if they don't understand the implications of each move, the project will be a disaster. You can have someone set the project up for them, but don't bother putting the final formulas into the spreadsheet until all the quotes are in. No matter how many times you tell them "don't move any columns" or "don't change any cells that have formulas in them", they <u>will</u> change them. That is a given. Once the "Main" or summary sheet is created, one simple sort on the "Breakout" page will change all the results to garbage. If you have just spent 300 hours on this project and the results are now useless, you are probably not going to be happy.

You will need someone with good reasoning and logic skills. When people get in the middle of a big spreadsheet they tend to lose sight of the final objective and get lost in the details. When that happens, they need to be able to think their way out of a problem. This spreadsheet, if done properly, will have 40 to 50 columns and one row for every piece part on the machine (500 to 2000) depending on the project. That is as many as 100,000 cells that need to be managed.

Did I mention that this is not for the faint of heart? If there is a question on a quote, they need to be able to find that quote among the hundreds and hundreds of quotes they have received. Suppliers don't always put the part number in the subject line of their email. It may only be a quote number and there may be 20 or 30 quotes from that one supplier. They also need to be able to use logic to see if they should question something. Can they spot something that doesn't pass the "logic test"? Will they investigate a part that "just doesn't look right"?

A competitive spirit is a good thing, too. That's what worked for me. I always wanted to have a better result on the current project than I had on the last one.

You will need someone with attention to detail. The easiest thing in the world is to put the information in the wrong cell or to type a number in wrong. Just misplace one decimal point and see what happens.

I was doing cost changes one time and missed the decimal point entirely. The part went from a price of $12.66825 each to $1,266,825.00 each. Okay, so it was only a <u>million dollar</u> variance! The sad part is that I didn't catch it and neither did our accounting department until the auditors came in. Suffice it to say, I learned my lesson.

Earlier, when I was discussing people that have worked at the same place for a long time, or are merely adequate employees, did that describe the person you were thinking of having do your project just because they are available? Or are they too "smart" to listen to a new way of doing business or too lazy to learn a complex new task? Those people are not going to give you a good result and if you spend the time and money to do a project like this, you want to have a good result – or more likely – a *great* result. If your best employee is too busy to do a project, it may be better to shift some of their work to someone else to free them up rather than give it to someone who won't do the best job possible just because they are available.

Once you have identified the need, established the rules, allocated the proper resources and have the information you need, you are ready to tackle the project.

## *Chapter 7 – How to Choose Your Target*

Now that you have decided that you have all your resources allocated, what should your project be? Depending on your company's product, size and goals, the target may vary. Here are some options.

### **By Machine**

If your company produces high cost, low volume products and you make more than eight or ten different products, you may want to look at your build schedule and see if you have several of one product coming up. Remember that a project takes two to three months to run plus the lead time for the parts to arrive, so look out at least that long. If you are going to make six of machine ABC, then your buying power is better if you can negotiate all six at once. If they are spread out over more than three months, you may need to negotiate with the suppliers in order to be able to buy them all at once and have them hold them or issue a blanket purchase order in order to get the better pricing.

If you look at the schedule six to nine months out and choose the machine you are going to make the most of, you can make that the first target. The next quarter, look six to nine months ahead and choose another one. You should be able to get four major projects each year.

Depending on how well you have reduced and contained costs in the past, you may see savings of $7,000.00 to $14,000.00 per machine per project. If your first project is six machines, your total savings could be $42,000.00 to $84,000.00. That is only your first project. If you do four projects a year, your savings could be over $300,000.00. Also, if you want to see the _actual_ savings, multiply the savings on each piece times the yearly usage. I think you will be pleasantly surprised!

## **By Production Line**

If your company produces high volume, low cost (under $500.00) products, you may want to look at the top three production lines. Create a list of all parts that are common (or similar) on the three lines and use that for your project.

### **By Supplier**

If neither of those works for you, you may want to look at your top suppliers, either by dollar value or by volume for your project. Whether by dollar value or volume, run a report that gives all the parts purchased from that supplier. If it is a long list, sort by price and use the top 20% for your project. The next quarter you can choose the next largest supplier for your project.

This also works well if you have a supplier that has had excessive cost increases or has historically had long lead times or short quote expiration dates.

### **By Commodity**

Another option is to do a project based on commodity. Choose a commodity, whether it's fabricated parts, electronic parts, cylinders, or any other area where you spend the majority of your budget and run a report on the parts. This will be your first project. The next quarter you can choose another commodity.

## **By Buyer**

You could even do a project by buyer. If you have a buyer that seems to have more price increases than other buyers, you could run a report on their purchase orders and use it for a project. Companies that assign each buyer a set of commodities may see more increases by one buyer than another because of the commodity they are buying. Or it may also be because that buyer isn't as conscientious as other buyers. You will have to decide which one is the cause.

No matter how you choose your project, the process is the same. The results are also going to be the same. The dollar values may be higher with some projects than others, but you will still see shorter lead times, longer quote expirations, lower economic batch quantities and higher inventory turns. How can you lose?

There is also another benefit I haven't mentioned. As you enter all the quotes into your ERP system at the end of the project, you will have more options available if the "best quote" has an issue or maybe they have a long lead time and you suddenly realize you need the part immediately. When you look at your notes, you will be able to tell at a glance if another supplier can get the part to you quicker. While price is _usually_ the motivating factor, we all know that sometimes lead time can be more important.

I can't tell you how many times I've paid more to expedite a part than the part cost to begin with. With all the other suppliers listed in the notes, you can call them and see if maybe, just maybe, they have one on the shelf.

Caution: When choosing your target project and the quantity to quote, I highly recommend choosing a _single quantity_ unless your people are _extremely skilled_ with Excel. Quoting quantities 5 _and_ 10 of a machine to see if you can do better with a higher quantity on parts that are quantity sensitive, but lower quantities of ones that aren't is a valid decision. The problem is that you don't just double the complexity of the project. It's more like triple. Most people struggle with the simpler (that's a relative term) spreadsheets of a single quantity. They can't even imagine how to begin setting up and running multiple quantities. Multiple quantities are not covered in this book, but once you have mastered the art of single quantities, multiples will become a bit easier.

## *Chapter 8 - Set Up*

How goes the set up, so goes the project. If you take extra care with the set up, the project will go more smoothly.

These are the headings you will want in your spreadsheet. If you put them into the spreadsheet in this order, the formulas provided now and later will work. You may want to shorten the headings. Since there are 45 columns in the initial spreadsheet, I have turned the column headings to a vertical position to fit them to the page. You will need to enter them horizontally and use "wrap text" and adjust them to the size you need to find the balance between having enough space to enter information and being able to get a reasonable amount of columns on your screen at one time.

If you have two large monitors for your computer, the projects are easier to do. They tend to take up a lot of "real estate" on your screen. At any given time, you will have your email, main cost reduction spreadsheet, your ERP system, your inventory query screen, supplier query screen, quoting spreadsheet, sample email sheets, drawings and drawing folders open. If you are doing your daily work at the same time, you may have another five or so screens open as well. Having 35 or more screens open at one time is not uncommon.

You may not need all the columns for your project; depending on where and how you get your information, but put them in the first time so the formulas you will be given will work. For later projects if you choose not to use all the columns you will have to adjust your formulas.

Rename the first "sheet" at the bottom. This one will be "Main". The second one will be named "Breakout". Until instructed otherwise, you will be working with the "Breakout" sheet.

**See "Excel Hint – Tabs" at the end of this book if you need help with this.**

After you have your initial spreadsheet setup with formulas, save it somewhere as a master to be used for all your projects. This will save time on future projects.

Once you have the "Master" saved, resave it with the title you want for your project. From this point on, remember "Save early and save often". If your spreadsheet gets lost because your computer crashes or you accidentally close it, you will be hard pressed to remember what information you put in since the last time you saved it. You will have to go back through the last emails and see if the information is in. Depending on how long since you last saved, this could waste an hour or more of time, not to mention the frustration involved.

Before you do any of the major re-sorts you will be doing, it is a good idea to hit save and then "Save As" to save the file with a new name each time. My file names look like this: "CR 86327 dumptruck 091813" where CR = Cost Reduction, 86327 = the machine number, dumptruck = the description and 091813 = the date of the spreadsheet. I use this formula (with two digits each for month, day and year) because I can always tell which the newest version is and when it was created. Excel won't allow a file name like 09/18/13, so this is the next best thing. You could also use 09-18-13 if that works better for you. The only thing to remember is to be consistent. If you do a "Save As" more than once in a day, you can use this format and just add "-1", "-2", etc. after the date.

If more than one person is working on this project at the same time, you will need to "share" the file. If that is the case, make sure everyone saves and closes the file before you do the "Save As". Otherwise, information will be lost and you will have no idea what it is or even that is it lost and that you should go looking for it.

You will notice that the title block on the very top of the spreadsheet will say "Shared" after the title once you have shared it.

**See "Excel Hint – Sharing" at the end of this book if you need help with this.**

Here is how your initial spreadsheet will be laid out.

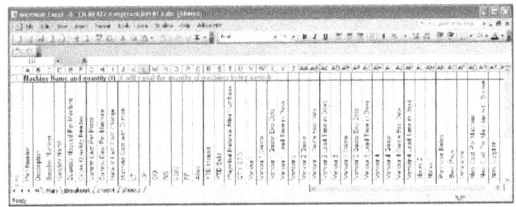

Column A = Part Number
Column B = Part Description

Column C = Supplier Number
Column D = Supplier Name
Column E = Quantity Needed Per Machine
Column F = Gross Quantity Needed - Quantity Needed Per Machine Multiplied by the Number of Machines Being Quoted
Column G = Current Cost Per Piece (Last Cost Entered)
Column H = Current Cost Per Machine
Column I = Date of Last Cost Change
Column J = Machine Cost With Burden
Column K = Current Lead Time (LT)
Column L = On Hand Quantity (OH)
Column M = On Order (OO)
Column N = Safety Stock (SS)
Column O = Economic Batch Quantity (EBQ)
Column P = Future Free (FF)
Column Q = Allocations (Alloc)
Column R = Year to Date Issued (YTD Issued)
Column S = Year to Date Sold (YTD Sold)
Column T = Net Quantity Needed
Column U = Quantity to Quote (QTY QTD)
Column V = Vendor 1
Column W = Vendor 1 Quote
Column X = Vendor 1 Quote Expiration Date

Column Y = Vendor 1 Lead Time in Days
Column Z = Vendor 2
Column AA = Vendor 2 Quote
Column AB = Vendor 2 Quote Expiration Date
Column AC = Vendor 2 Lead Time in Days
Column AD = Vendor 3
Column AE = Vendor 3 Quote
Column AF = Vendor 3 Quote Expiration Date
Column AG = Vendor 3 Lead Time in Days
Column AH = Vendor 4
Column AI = Vendor 4 Quote
Column AJ = Vendor 4 Quote Expiration Date
Column AK = Vendor 4 Lead Time in Days
Column AL = Notes 2
Column AM = Notes 1
Column AN = Purchase notes
Column AO = Best Price
Column AP = Difference
Column AQ = New Cost Per Machine
Column AR = New Cost Per Machine with Burden
Column AS = New Supplier

## NEW SPREADSHEET SET UP

Before you start worrying about formulas, a good first step is to freeze the panes on your spreadsheet so the headers are always available. This makes it easier to get the information into the right cells. You will be able to scroll down until the part you want is the first part visible.

**See "Excel Hint – Freeze panes" at the end of this book if you need help with this.**

For the explanations and formulas, I will refer to the Columns by their letter designations. Not all columns will need further explanation. For the formulas, "X" will be used for the number of machines being quoted. Any Columns that are not specifically called out below are either self explanatory or the information will come directly from your ERP software or Bill of Materials.

**See "Excel Hint – Formulas" at the end of this book if you need help with this.**

Columns:

F) Gross quantity is calculated by multiplying the Quantity Per Machine times the Number of Machines being quoted. Formula for the first row is written as:

**=E3*X**
**(X=number of machines being quoted)**

H) Current cost per machine is calculated by multiplying Quantity Per Machine times Current Cost Per Piece. Formula for the first row is written as:

**=G3*E3**

J) Machine Cost with Burden. If you use burdened costs for your project, this is where you would calculate the burdened cost. Formula for the first row is written as:

**=H3*Y**
**(Y equals your company's burden rate)**

R and S) Adding "year to date issued" and "year to date sold" together will give you total annual usage for that part.

T) Net Quantity Needed - This column is for the "Net" quantity needed. As opposed to Column F which is "Gross" quantity needed, this column will calculate how many you actually need based on current values. If you have a negative number, you will be short parts. If you have a positive number, you will have a surplus and probably don't need to quote the part. Note that this is only a snapshot. By the time the project is finished, these values will change but it gives you a good basis for estimating "Net" quantity needed. Formula for the first row is written as:

**=P3-F3-N3**

## *Chapter 9 – Evaluation*

U) Quantity to Quote - Using Columns G, K, L, M, N, O, P, Q, R, S, T and AM, evaluate how many you actually want to quote. Notice that columns G, R and S are included in this evaluation. A very inexpensive part with high usage may be more cost effective to quote a higher quantity in order to order less often. For a very expensive part you may want to order just the minimum. Be sure to take into account the physical size of the part. If you buy a dozen extra 12 foot long parts because you got a better price, but have no place to store them, you didn't gain anything.

Your objective here is to find the *best price* on the *smallest quantity* you can buy without risking *running out* or having to order the same part every *two days*. Simple, right? Well, maybe not, but it gets easier with practice. Keep in mind that two different people reviewing this may come up with two different numbers because it is somewhat subjective.

AN) - Purchasing Notes - If you use purchasing notes in your ERP system, they will be very helpful in this process. It could save you time quoting something that was just quoted or keep you from trying to requote something to more suppliers that is a single source part.

AM) - Notes 1 - Use this column to make any new notes, such as manufacturers name (Vickers, Eaton, Allen Bradley, etc.), revision change, possible new suppliers to quote, or any other information that will be useful once you start sending requests for quotes so you don't have to go back and wade through the entire note every time.

These columns will get you the information you need in order to start quoting. You can now hide any of the columns you are through using. NOTE: DO NOT DELETE these columns and DO NOT MOVE them. You will need to unhide them during the process to verify or reevaluate information as questions arise, but for now, they are better off out of the way.

**See "Excel Hint – Hide and Unhide" at the end of this book if you need help with this.**

If you are working from a Bill of Material (BOM) and have to create the spreadsheet by hand, it will take much longer to do, but it can be done.

You can skip this section and go directly to Chapter 10 if you have access to a parts list that is already broken down into components. If you are working from a Bill of Materials, you will need to follow this section.

**How to Breakdown a BOM**

If you have to create the entire spreadsheet manually from the BOM, start by pulling the main drawing. On the spreadsheet, list all the parts shown in the BOM on the drawing. The beginning of the spreadsheet will look like this:

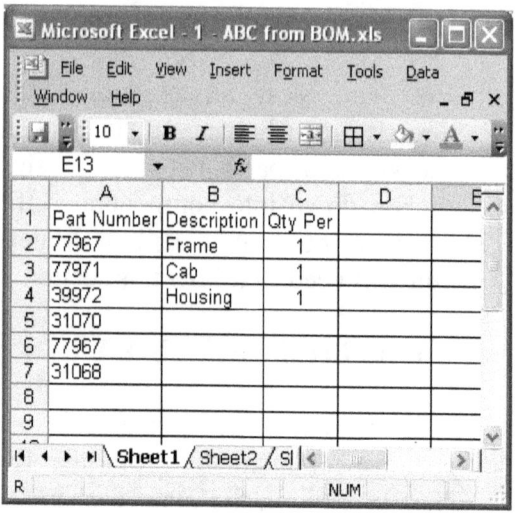

As you enter the part number from the drawing, add the description of the part and the quantity needed per machine. Next, pull the drawing for the first part (PN 77967). In this case, the first part has several sub parts. Insert lines for each sub part and list the sub part numbers and descriptions on those lines.

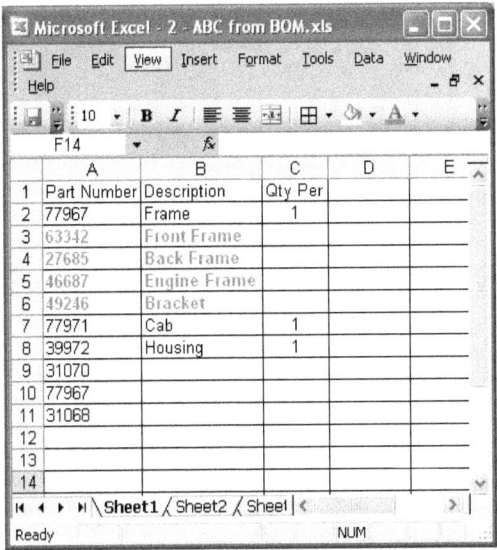

Notice the highlighted parts have been added to the list. Now take a look at the drawing for the first sub part (PN 63342). Insert lines for each sub part in this sub part.

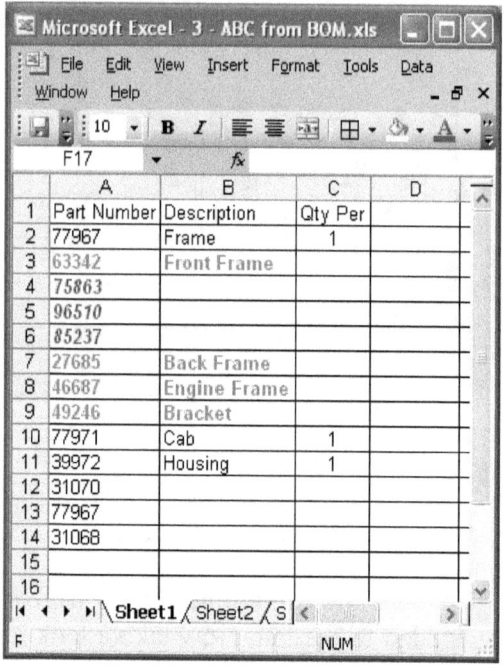

Notice the newly added lines. Continue this process of breaking down each part until you have a complete list of parts for the machine. You will have some parts that are used in more than one place. List them each time they appear and enter the description and quantity. When there are no more parts to break down, you will have your list created for the cost reduction.

At this point, you will want to sort your spreadsheet by part number and combine any duplicates. Add these quantities together and then delete the extra lines.

This is the same process you will use when you start pulling drawings for quote packages. If you have a part that has sub parts, you will need to set up a folder for the part (PN 77967) with sub folders for the sub parts (PN 63342, 27685, PN 46687 and PN 49246). If any of the next level parts need to be broken down, they will need folders made as well. Once this spreadsheet is complete you can add your columns and formulas to make it match the spreadsheet in Chapter 8.

## *Chapter 10 – Quoting*

Now that you have determined how many of each part you want to quote, it is time to start the quoting process.

For this part of the process, you will use Columns A through D, G, V, Z. AD, AH, AL, and AM. Notice that all of Vendor 1 information is highlighted in blue; Vendor 2 is highlighted in yellow; etc. You can use any color you wish, but it does help to have them highlighted in different colors to make putting the information in the right place easier. Also, the entire first column of each "Vendor" block is in red. As the spreadsheet starts to get populated with information, having the vendor number in red keeps it separate from the other information.

Your new spreadsheet with only the needed columns visible will look like this. This is much easier to manage.

Your first step will be to sort the spreadsheet by column G – Current Cost Per Piece

**See "Excel Hint – Sorting" at the end of this book if you need help with this.**

You will probably not want to quote any parts that cost less than $2.00. The payback is generally not worth the work.

Move all the parts that are less than $2.00 down to the bottom of the spreadsheet. Insert a row and label it as "Under $2.00".

Now you will want to do a multiple sort of all the parts above the "Under $2.00" line by C – Supplier Number and then B - Description. This will help you put your quote requests together in groups for easier quoting.

**See "Excel Hint – Multiple Sort" at the end of this book if you need help with this.**

As you go through the process, it will be helpful to resort by other values in order to be able to group similar parts together. Quoting all springs or cylinders or valves at the same time is easier than doing a spring and then a cylinder and then back to springs, etc. If you can send out a dozen parts on one email instead of one part on a dozen emails, it saves a lot of time.

You will need to pull drawings to send with each part you quote. The easiest way to collect drawings is to set up temporary folders on your desktop. If it is a medium to large project (more than 100 line items) you will need to set up several folders. You might want to name them Drawings 1, Drawings 2, etc. or name them by type of part such as Drawings Fabricated, Drawings Electrical, Drawings Hydraulic. Use whatever groupings work for your project. If you have parts in the grouping that are made of several other parts, you will need to make a sub folder within the main folder for each of these type parts.

**See "Excel Hint – Set up Folders" at the end of this book if you need help with this.**

Identify small groups of parts to quote at one time and choose where you will quote them. It is generally good to include the original vendor of record as one of the vendors to quote. Try to quote at least three (four if possible) vendors for each part. This will not always be possible because some parts may be single source or proprietary.

As you pull the drawings (and all the sub assembly and sub sub assembly drawings) put them in the appropriate folder on your desktop. As you send the drawings and request for quote (RFQ) out put the supplier number in the appropriate cell for the supplier you are quoting. This way you can track where you have sent RFQs so you know who to contact later when you are chasing missing quotes.

If you don't already have a "Supplier Cheat Sheet" I would highly recommend creating one as you do your first project. You may know automatically where you can quote the majority of parts because you deal with them frequently. But for the remaining parts you will have to research a little to find the right suppliers to quote. The next time you come across a similar part, will you remember who can supply it? Probably not if you are dealing with a large project. That's where the "Supplier Cheat Sheet" can help. Open a blank spreadsheet, name it and save it somewhere handy. In the first column put a heading for "Brand" and further down a heading for "Commodity". Below the "Brand" heading start listing the brands you use such as Eaton, Honeywell, Martin, Murr, etc. and who can supply them. Do the same with "Commodities" for hoses, hardware, wire, cylinders, machined, etc. For each line item, enter the supplier name and then the supplier number of all the people that can supply that part. Keep adding to it as you find more parts. This is also a great tool for your next project and for your daily work as well. It will look like this:

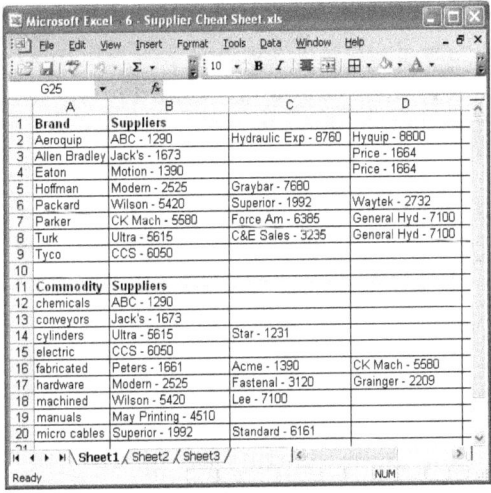

Later in the project when you are ready to start chasing quotes it is a good idea to set up a separate spreadsheet for tracking who you have contacted.

It will look something like this:

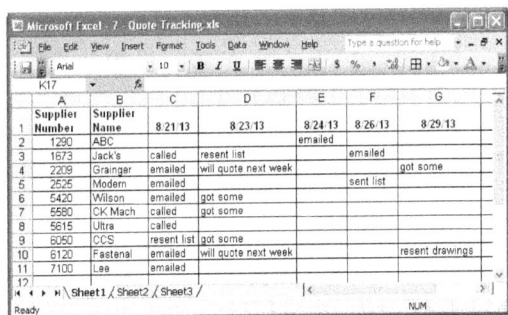

In Outlook (or other email program) you will want to set up a sub folder in your Outbox and one in your Inbox for the project you are working on. Give it a name that will easily identify it for future reference. It could be "CR 71853 dumptruck" in which the CR = Cost Reduction, the 71853 = the part number of the upper level machine or part and "dumptruck" is a description of the machine. As you send requests and receive quotes, it is helpful to drag the emails to these folders. If your email highlights unread messages in bold, and you do a search, the "bold" may be lost and you will think you already addressed that email. If you move it as soon as it is dealt with, you will know for sure you entered the information in the spreadsheet. This way it doesn't matter if the email looks like its read or not, you will still know if you have entered the information in the spreadsheet. The other advantage is that it makes it easier to find an email if you need to verify that the request was sent or review the quote when questions arise. And, believe me, they _will_ arise. This will also keep them segregated from the hundreds of emails you get as part of your other job duties.

Depending on your company policy, you may want to save all the incoming and outgoing emails into a shared folder at the end of each project so everyone can access them. If they are already in a folder, it's easy to move them to the new shared folder.

As you receive quotes, you will see some that quote a deviation from the print. Depending on your company policy, you will probably want to evaluate some of these deviations. If it is an <u>increase</u> or a <u>very small decrease</u>, it isn't worth the effort. If it is a good savings, you may want to have the engineers review to see if it's acceptable. Put a note in the "Notes 2" column saying that you have requested the evaluation. When you are inputting your notes into the ERP system at the end, this is something you will want to make note of. If the substitute is approved, make a note of that, along with the date of approval and person who approved it. If it is not approved, make that note as well to save time the next time this part gets quoted. If you are waiting for approval, put that in the notes along with who is evaluating the substitute.

Notice the difference between the "Notes 1" and "Notes 2" columns. "Notes 1" is used for inputting information that will help you with quoting process. "Notes 2" is for inputting information that will go into your ERP system or help explain a quote when the project is finished.

Remember that as you are receiving emails with all the quotes you have requested, you will still be getting emails about other parts you are quoting for your daily work and various other emails in general. To help distinguish the cost reduction emails from other quotes, it helps to use something like "CR" as the beginning of your Subject line in your email followed by the part number or grouping designation. Most suppliers will use the "CR" designation on their quote or email, but some won't. For the ones that do, bless their little hearts. For the ones that don't, well, you tried. Take what you can get and be happy.

**SENDING REQUEST FOR QUOTE**

Open a new email and enter the name of the person you want to send the quote to. In the subject line, put "CR" and the part number or other identifier. Ask for price, lead time and quote expiration date. Give the quantity or quantities required. Any RFQ must have drawings attached. All sub drawings must also be included.

Here is an example of the email asking for quotes.

> *We are doing a cost reduction project on our ABC machine. Please provide price, lead time and quote expiration date for the following as soon as possible. We will be buying these in fourth quarter. Please try to hold your pricing at least until the end of the year. Please reference our part number on all quotes.*
>
> *If the drawing says "or equal" you may quote a sub, but please **<u>note that it is a sub</u>** and give the specs for the suggested part. If it does not say "or equal" please do not quote a sub.*
>
> *If there are other quantities that make economic sense, feel free to quote those as well as the quantity asked for.*

Then list the part numbers and quantities you want quoted or attach a "block" spreadsheet (explained below) and attach the appropriate drawings and send your email.

When you are quoting this way, the suppliers will know that these are going to be real orders that are going to be placed very soon and will give them a higher priority.

By the way, this is also good information to put on your quotes for your daily work. It's not just for projects.

You may or may not need all three paragraphs shown above depending on the situation. If you open a Word document and type in the message you are going to use, you can copy and paste the message for each email you send. It saves a lot of time and makes sure you don't miss any of the important information you want to send.

**See "Excel Hint – Attach Files" at the end of this book if you need help with this.**

If you are sending the same RFQ to multiple suppliers, you can "forward" the email after you send it. Go to your email "sent" folder and open the email you just sent. Select "forward". Remove the "FW" in the subject box and the original signature and any other unwanted information. Add the desired person in the "To" box. Send the email.

The easiest way to get more work done in less time is to set up "blocks" of similar parts to quote, especially if they are all going to be sent to the same vendors. This will require some sorting and resorting of your spreadsheet, but is well worth the effort.

As you prepare to send out the "blocks", open a blank Excel sheet and copy / paste each small group into the new spreadsheet. Then delete the columns you don't want the suppliers to see. It can then be attached to the email. This saves retyping the list with the quantities for each email. You will want to add a column for their price, the expiration date and the lead time so the supplier only needs to fill in the blanks. Some will fill out the spreadsheet and some will send a formal quote in their own format. Either way, you only care about the information they give you, not how they give it, but it is easier to deal with information that is already in the same format as you are using.

If suppliers don't provide all the information, you will need to send it back requesting the missing information. Typically, the majority of the suppliers will send the price, and either the lead time or the quote expiration date, but not all three the first time. As they get used to you sending the emails back and asking for more information, they will start supplying the information in the first email. Be patient; it's just a matter of training them.

If they do put an expiration date on the quote, but it isn't very far out, go back to them and ask for three or six months – or longer. Many suppliers will extend their expiration dates if you explain what you are doing and when you will be placing purchase orders. Also, after you explain that some suppliers are agreeing to extend their expiration dates, more will join in.

A few companies will not put your part number on the quote, only theirs. If you only have a few parts from that supplier, you can probably figure out which part they are quoting. If you have a large number of parts, it will be very difficult. Again, after you send a few quotes back asking for more information they will start supplying it the first time.

Also, sometimes a number gets transposed when they send the quote back. You ask for part number 78623 and they send the quote calling it part number 76823. This will need a follow up phone call or email to verify that they meant part number 78623. For these I prefer email because it gives me a record if I need to go back and verify information. Generally, you are already pretty sure what part they meant, but it is best to verify rather than have them say later that they never quoted the part. Besides, it will give them a chance to correct the part number in their system so they recognize it when you place the order.

If the drawings are too large to email or there are too many to email, you may have to compress or "Zip" them first.

**See "Excel Hint – Zip Files" at the end of this book if you need help with this.**

Another option for large files is a File Transfer Protocol (FTP) site. This will need the help of your IT department to set up and then you will have to contact the vendors that are going to be using it and give them the log in and password information.

Columns:

Vendor (V, Z, AD and AH) - As you send out requests, these are the columns you will use for the vendor number. If possible, it is better to use the vendor number rather than the vendor name for a couple reasons. The vendor number is generally shorter and as the project expands, space on your computer screen comes at a premium. Also, this helps avoid confusion if you have more than one supplier that has a similar name, such as Jack's Electrical Supply, and Jack's Electronics. If you only put "Jack's" in the cell (because that is all that fits) you may get them confused later.

You will want to format the cells in these columns to "Number" with "0" decimal places. Caution: only format one column at a time. If you highlight V, Z, AD and AN all together, you will be formatting all the hidden cells in between. You can, however, hold the control key down while you individually select only the columns you want to format.

**See "Excel Hint – Format Cells" at the end of this book if you need help with this.**

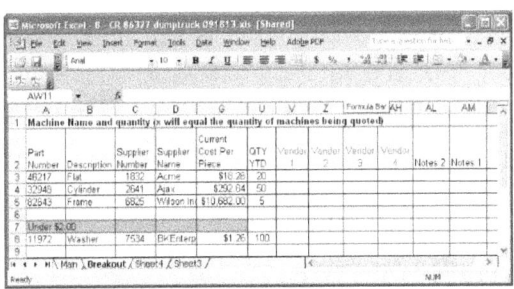

As you start getting quotes in, you will need to put them in the spreadsheet. At this point, unhide columns V through AK.

You will want to format the cells as follows:

All "Quote" Columns (W, AA, AE, AI) – format as a "Number" with "2" decimal places. For some parts, you may need to change the individual cells to four or five decimal places, but to begin with, two will work well.

All "Exp" Columns (X, AB, AF, AJ) – format as a "Date" with 3/14/01 format. This is the shortest format that you can use and still get all the information you need. Like I mentioned earlier, space becomes important very quickly.

All "LT" columns (Y, AC, AG, AK) – format as a "Number" with "0" decimal places. Usually lead times will be entered in days. Most quotes come in with lead times in weeks. Whether your company uses working days or calendar days, be sure to convert lead times to the appropriate days. Your quotes will often come in with the lead times as a range, say "2-4 weeks". It is a matter of company policy if you are going to enter the minimum or the maximum number of days, but generally you are better off to list the maximum. By doing this, reports that flag long lead time items will pull the longer date. If you can get it sooner it is all the better. You just don't want to find out that it won't come in until much later than you thought. Always err on the side of caution.

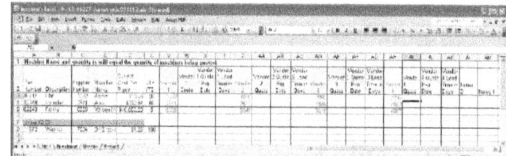

Notice in the screen shot above that the cell AI3 is highlighted. Whatever cell you have clicked on will have the row (row 3) and the column (column AI) highlighted in orange in the border. As the spreadsheet gets bigger and you have more information to input, this little trick will help you. Because the part number is right next to the highlighted row 3, you can verify that you are, indeed, putting the quote in the correct row for that part number. It looks pretty simple now, but look at it after just a few quotes are input. Notice that the same cell is highlighted, but now it's not as obvious.

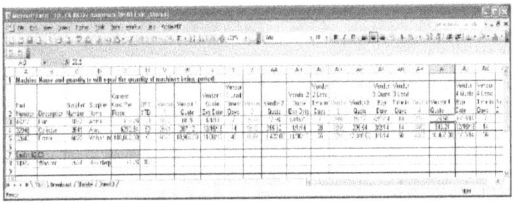

Another simple trick to help stay on the correct line is to always have the line you are examining or inputting information into on the very top of the spreadsheet. That will make the header line your guideline and help keep you from inputting information in the wrong cell. If you have frozen rows 1 and 2, you only need to scroll up or down until your target row is in position.

This part of the process will take six to eight weeks depending on several factors such as: how much time you have to spend on it, how quickly the suppliers get back to you, how many parts are on the list and how good your vendor base is. If you have several qualified suppliers for each commodity, you won't have to go searching for more suppliers in order to get three suppliers to quote.

After your quotes are entered, you can hide the "Exp" and "LT" columns to shorten the spreadsheet. Unhide columns "AO", "AP" and "AS".

It will look like this:

You are now ready to find out how well you did. Finally! Results! It's what you have spent the last two or three months trying to get to!

AO) Still using the original "Breakout" sheet, your first step is to calculate the "Best Price". Formula for the first row is written as:

**=MIN(W3,AA3,AE3,AI3)**

Note that all formulas must be put in exactly as they appear. If you add a space or miss a comma you will not get the answer you are looking for.

AP) Next you will calculate the "Difference". The formula for the first row is written as:

**=G3-AO3**

Note that a negative number means an increase and a positive number means a decrease. The easy way to remember that is "Negative is bad".

AS) The next step is to calculate the "New Supplier". The formula for the first row is written as:

**=IF(AO3=W3,V3,IF(AO3=AA3,Z3,IF(AO3=AE3,AD3,IF(AO3=AI3,AH3)))**

You will want to copy the formulas to all the cells below them and then calculate a sum. Starting at the first cell below the heading, right click on the lower right hand corner of the cell and drag it down. This will copy the formula to all the cells. Go back to the top of the spreadsheet and click on that first cell with a formula and highlight it – and all the cells below it. Keep highlighting until you are past the last formula by two cells. With all the cells still highlighted, go to the tool bar on Excel and click on the "sum" symbol. It looks like this: $\Sigma$ . If that doesn't work, you can put in a formula. Click on the second blank cell below the last row you want to sum.

AP) For "Difference" the sum formula is written as:

**=SUM(AP3:AP6)**

In this case, the "AP6" would be the row number of the last cell you want included in your sum. Since every spreadsheet will have a different number of rows, the number in the last part of this formula will change every time.

After you have the first formula calculated, you can copy / paste it to other cells where you want a similar sum. Excel will recalculate the formula based on the new columns you are using.

Unhide all columns and then rehide everything except A, B, C, D, E, G, H, J, U, V, W, Z, AA, AD, AE, AH, AI, AL, AO, AP, AQ, AR, and AS

Your spreadsheet will look like this.

It's time for more formulas.

AQ) For "New Cost Per Machine" the first line of the formula would be written as:

**=AO3*E3**

AR) For "New cost Per Machine with Burden" the first line of the formula would be written as:

**=AQ3*Y**

Again, for this formula, "Y" equals the burden rate your company uses. This does not refer to column Y.

This is what your spreadsheet will look like now.

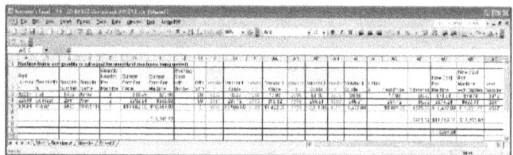

Subtract the total in column AQ from the total in column H. In this case the result is a positive $287.64. Since it is a *positive* number that is how much you *saved* per machine.

For the saving the first line of the formula would be written as:

**=H7-AQ7**

Your new spreadsheet will look like this:

Notice that this new total does not match the total in cell AP7. That is because the total in cell AQ9 takes into account the quantities needed and the total in cell AQ7 is based on price per piece. In the spreadsheet for a full project, these two numbers won't be as close and it will be less confusing.

This one formula gives you the information you have worked so hard for so long to get. Pat yourself on the back and enjoy a moment of victory.

If you stop here, you will still probably have an *adequate* project. If you want a *stellar* project, you will take it to the next level.

Use the AP column to find more places to save money.

Look for any parts that have a negative number. See if there are more places you can send to for a quote. If you have run out of columns, put the information in column AL (Notes 2). Just remember that the formulas won't pull information from this column. You will need to address it individually. If they are the lowest bidder, the best way to address this is to move the information from the spreadsheet for a supplier that was a no quote (or a higher quote if necessary) to the "Notes 2" column and replace it with the information for the new supplier. Just remember that when you are entering all the notes into your ERP system when the project is finished, you need to address the information in the "Notes 2" column as well as in the main body of the spreadsheet.

You also want to go back to suppliers that have an increase and see if they will hold their price for the next purchase. Surprisingly, many of them will.

Look at any part that has a different supplier listed in column AS from the original supplier listed in column C. They may be willing to lower their price to keep from losing the part.

Review the spreadsheet to see if there is anything that doesn't pass the "logic test". Look at the quotes you have. Ask yourself if each piece makes sense. Example: Three suppliers quote around $200.00 for a part. One supplier shows a quote of $20.00. Chances are there was a typo when you entered the information, a typo when the supplier entered the information or the supplier missed something or misunderstood the part. Your formulas will pick this up as a very big (however inaccurate) savings if you don't catch it.

Depending on the number of line items you have, this part of the project will take a week or more to review and requote. If you have done well with your final review, your savings should have increased.

Your "Detail" sheet is now complete.

## Chapter 11 - Summary Evaluation

The easiest way I have found to create the "Main" or Summary page is to copy / paste all of the "Breakout" sheet into the "Main" spreadsheet and then delete what you don't want from the "Main" sheet. DO NOT DELETE any information on the "Breakout" Sheet. That is why we don't start with a blank sheet and set up the formulas ahead of time. A word of caution here: Once you copy / paste the information into the "Main" if you delete or move a row on the "Breakout" sheet all your formulas will be skewed. Also, when you copy / paste to the "Main" sheet, your formulas will not be carried over. You will only be able to carry over the results of the formula.

To copy, go to the "Breakout" sheet, highlight all columns and rows by clicking on the very upper left corner of the spreadsheet. It will be the cell to the left of column A and above the cell for row 1. Right click on this cell. Then select "copy". Now click on the "Main" tab and then right click on the corresponding upper left corner of the spreadsheet. Then select "paste". Your "Main" sheet will now look exactly like your "Breakout" sheet.

This is a really great time to do a "Save As" and give the file name a new date. This way if you make an error, you at least have the original information in a safe form to fall back on.

On the "Main" sheet you will want to unhide all columns and then delete (Yes, I actually said you would delete something!) all columns except the following:

Part Number
Description
Supplier Number
Qty Per Machine
Current Cost Per Piece

Notice I didn't use the letter designations for the columns in this explanation because every time you delete a column, the designations for remaining columns will change.

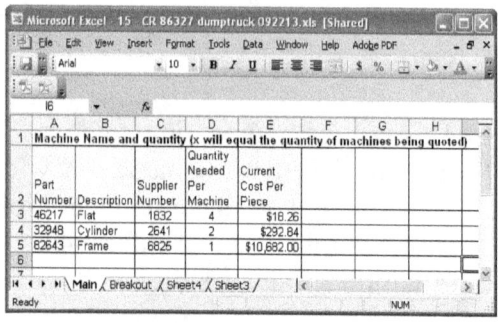

You will now have the following new columns in your "Main" page.

A) Part Number
B) Description
C) Supplier Number
D) Quantity Per Machine
E) Current Cost Per Piece

Next add the following columns:

F) Current Cost Per Machine
G) Machine Cost with Burden
H) New Supplier
I) Best Price
J) New Cost Per Machine
K) New Cost Per Piece with Burden
L) Total Burdened Cost Per Unit

Your new spreadsheet should look like this.

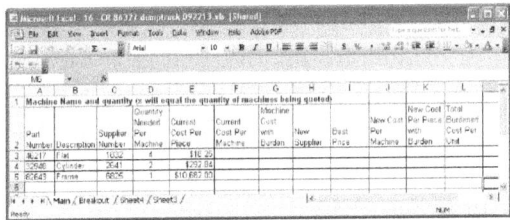

Notice that we didn't carry forward all the information in the columns except "A" through "E". We will bring that information forward with formulas. That way if you change a price on the "Breakout" sheet, it will automatically update the "Main" sheet if it is a new "best" price and/or the new vendor if that changes. This is very important because you will want to do any changes on the "Breakout" sheet *not* on the "Main" sheet. Let me remind you that if you change the location of a row or column or delete a row or column after the "Main" is created, you will skew the numbers.

Here are your next formulas for the "Main" sheet.

F) Current Cost Per Machine – the formula for the first cell is written as:

=D3*E3

G) Machine Cost With Burden – the formula for the first cell is written as:

**=F3\*Y**
**"Y" = burden rate**

H) New Supplier – the formula for the first cell is written as:

**=Breakout!AS3**

I) Best Price – the formula for the first cell is written as:

**=Breakout!AO3**

J) New Cost Per Machine – the formula for the first cell is written as:

**=Breakout!AQ3**

K) New Cost Per Piece with Burden – the formula for the first cell is written as:

**=D3\*J3**

L) Total Burdened Cost Per Unit – the formula for the first cell is written as:

**=Breakout!AR3**

Drag all these formulas down to the last line of your project just as you did for the "Breakout" sheet. Review the spreadsheet to make sure there are no cells that say "0" or "FALSE" or something else other than a number. If there are, these need to be corrected before you continue.

Now do a sum for column "G" and also for column "L" two spaces below the last line like you did for the "Breakout" sheet.

In the space two cells below your total in column L enter the following formula:

**=G7-L7**

Again, you will have to adjust your formula to account for the number of lines in your spreadsheet, but it is basically the total in column G minus the total in column L.

Did you notice that your savings before were $287.34 and now they are $319.28. How can that be? The $287.34 came from the actual costs. The $318.95 came from the burdened cost.

Your new spreadsheet will look like this:

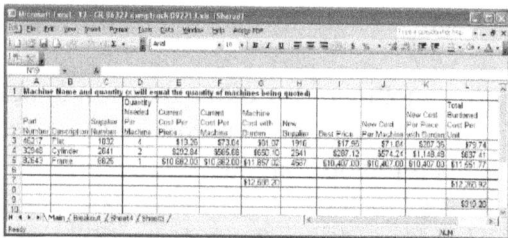

Now you will add the Summary Block. After your totals, create two blocks that look like the ones in the next diagram. Make sure they are in the same relative position. There are two blank rows between the totals and the "Target" information. The "Target" starts in column B. In the "real" world, the number of spaces between items really doesn't matter. The only reason it matters here is in order to show how the formulas work.

For this exercise, we will use the burdened costs. If you want to use the unburdened costs, you can adjust the formulas to those cells. Also, because formulas are based on individual cells and because the total number of lines will vary from project to project, I will set the formulas based on this spreadsheet.

Since the totals are on row 7 in this example, you will have to subtract 7 from the row number of your own totals and add that number to each formula you are given. Example: Your spreadsheet totals are on line 588. Subtract 7 from 588 to get your factor of 581. You will, therefore, add 581 to each formula given. In the formula =K22/K20 you would add 581 to each number and get this formula: =K603/K601.

Information for the left, or "Target" block, will be provided for you by management. Make a note of who gave you the target and the date they gave it to you. It will make it much easier to go back and look up the email or your notes if the need arises.

The information for the right, or "Actual" block is what we are concerned with here. Notice we don't start at the top.

Cell K12 the formula is written as:

**=G7**

Cell K13 the formula is written as:

**=L7**

Cell K14 the formula is written as:

**=K12-K13**

Cell K16 the formula is written as:

**=E14-K14**

Cell K11 the formula is written as:

**=K14/K12**

In a real project, your amount "Remaining" will more than likely be much closer to the target, or even a negative number, which means you saved more than the target. Your spreadsheet will now look like this.

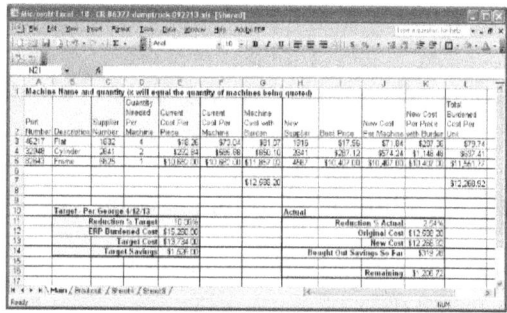

Save the file one last time and then do a "Save As" and use the current date and put the word "final" in the name after the date.

At this point your project will probably be presented to management for review.

The last step is to input all the information you have gathered into your ERP system's notes section and change vendor, lead time and economic batch quantity information as needed. Whether you change the pricing information in your system is dependent on your company policy. Your accounting department may be in charge of that. Your part of this may take a week or two. That sounds like a long time, but keep in mind that you may have 100,000 pieces of information to input and copy / paste will not help you here. It has to be entered manually and the changes need to be made manually. I recommend a short nap followed by a large cup of coffee before you begin. This is very tedious work but accuracy is more important than speed. If you type in the wrong information, you may find yourself spending a lot of time looking for the original quotes for that part in order to correct your mistake.

I would suggest that you put notes in your ERP system and have them laid out like this:

> CR 86327 Dumptruck
> Was Ajax at $xx.xx
> Quantity quoted – 5
> Acme = $xx.xx, exp 12/1/12, LT 7
> Ajax = $xx.xx, exp 11/12/12, LT 21

The first line should be the title of your project. This will help narrow down where to look for the quotes if you need to find one later.

The second line is who the original supplier was and their original price. If the supplier didn't change, you can skip this line.

The third line is the quantity quoted.

The fourth line is the quote from the successful bidder starting with the supplier, then the price, then the expiration date of the quote and then the lead time in days. By always putting the successful quote first you can save time later by not having to read all the information unless something changes with the first bidder. With this format, the new price is always right next to the supplier name.

All other quotes will be listed next in whatever order you choose, but follow the same format as the successful quote.

When all the information is entered, enter the current date and your name and save the notes.

Next, you will need to go into your ERP system and make changes to the supplier, lead time, EBQ and possibly pricing – depending on your company policy.

Again, depending on company policy, you may want to mark any parts for QC inspection if the vendor changed. This way the first parts will be checked prior to being put on the shelf. This gives you time to address any issues before the part is needed. If you wait until the part is needed and then discover there is an issue, it becomes a rush situation.

After the notes and changes are complete, go back to the spreadsheet and change the entire row for that part to a different color to show it's complete. Then scroll down so that line is hidden under the title line and the next now you're going to address is at the top.

Since you won't be able to do all of this part in one day, changing the color helps keep track of where you left off. Also, if you find something you want to investigate further you can simply skip that row and keep doing input. Because you don't change the color of any lines you skip, they will be easy to spot when you are ready to go back and investigate them.

## Chapter 12 - Cost Containment

Now that you have worked hard to reduce your costs on a machine or a production line, you want to make sure that those costs, as well as others, don't increase over time. You also want to make sure that you are buying the *correct parts* at the *correct price* and for the *correct lead time*. This is where the Cost Containment project comes in. Even if you have chosen not to do a Cost Reduction project, the Cost Containment project can benefit you.

**What you want to achieve**

The first thing on your list is probably to make sure you are *holding* pricing on your parts. If every cost increase is scrutinized and explained, only the truly unavoidable increases will be allowed.

You need a way to make sure there weren't typos in entering the purchase order. If the buyer wanted to buy part number 82653 and accidentally typed 82563, it may not get caught right away otherwise.

You want to make sure large or expensive items aren't ordered with higher quantities than needed. If you aren't going to use the extra pieces for a year or more, you are going to be paying to inventory them. I have seen parts with an EBQ of 200 and no safety stock have a future free quantity of 800. With a Cost Containment project, the increased order would have been caught and cancelled.

But how can you do all this without hiring more people? Ah, the power of reports and spreadsheets. That's how.

Just a caution here – it is best to have a third party do this part. If the person reviewing the purchase orders is the same person that issued them, they may take short cuts. Believing that all their information is correct, they may just copy and past the information into the spreadsheet and not really investigate. Remember, part of this exercise is to catch mistakes. It's best not the have the fox watching the hen house.

Before you can start you will have to have someone create a report writer that will capture the initial information you need. This will be the beginning of your Daily PO Review. Whoever does the maintenance on your ERP system or one of your IT people should be able to create this. Here is the information you are going to request as output from the report writer.

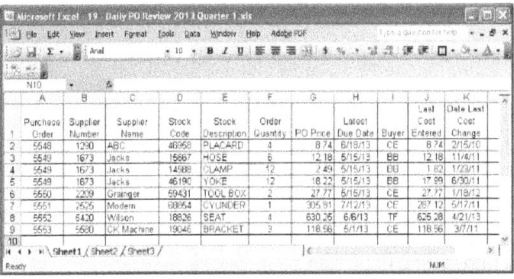

Here are the columns:

A) Purchase Order
B) Supplier Number
C) Supplier Name
D) Stock code or part number
E) Stock code (or part number) description
F) Order quantity of purchase order
G) Purchase Order price
H) Latest due date of this line item
I) Buyer initials or name
J) Last Cost Entered (current price shown in your ERP system)
K) Date Last Cost Change

This is the information that will be automatically input into the spreadsheet when you run the report that has been created. The first time you run the report, you will want to save it to a folder named

"Daily PO Review" with sub folders for the current year and the current quarter. The file name would be: Daily PO Review 2013 Quarter 1. You will save it in a sub folder named "Daily PO Review 1st Quarter 2013".

This file will be saved with a date at the end every time the report is run. The file needs to be shared so other people can input their responses to your questions.

As you start reviewing, you will want to eliminate any line items that do not fall under the heading of parts you want to investigate. There will be purchase orders for services, business cards, and other non-manufacturing items. You can just delete them, but it is better to use "Sheet 2" and cut / paste the line items to that. This way, all the purchase orders and line items can be accounted for if a review is needed.

Each quarter you will want to start a new file and place it in the appropriate folder. This is a running report, so all entries for the entire quarter will be visible in one file. After the first file is created for the quarter, each time you run the report, you will want to input the information into a blank Excel file first and then copy / paste the information into your Daily PO Review file.

After you save the first file for the first quarter, you will want to add some columns to your spreadsheet. Again, in order to make this view large enough to be legible I have compressed the headings. The headings in yellow are the ones that will have the information imported automatically. The balance you will have to be input manually.

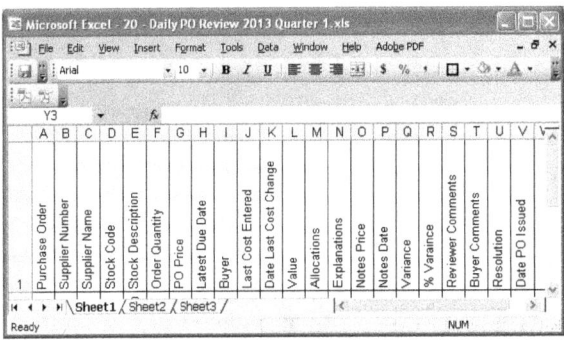

The additional columns will be:

L) Total line value
M) Allocations
N) Explanation
O) Notes Price
P) Notes Date
Q) Variance
R) % Variance
S) Reviewer comments
T) Buyer comments
U) Resolution

V) Date PO Issued

Here are the explanations and formulas:

Column L – Total line value. The formula for the first cell is written as:

**=G2*F2**

Column M - Allocations (what caused the need for a purchase order to be issued – specifically, what machine build or production line is it needed for)

Column N - Explanation (for additional notes)

Column O - Notes Price (what your current notes in the ERP system say the price is) Note: this will not always be the same as the information pulled in automatically).

Column P - Notes Date (date that the notes on new pricing were input). This column should be formatted as "Date - 3/17/12".

Column Q - Variance (difference between Last Cost Entered and the PO Price). A negative number is a price increase. A positive is a price reduction. Remember –negative is bad. The formula for the first cell is written as:

$$=J2-G2$$

Column R - % Variance (percentage difference between Last Cost Entered and the PO Price). This column should be formatted as "Percentage – 2 decimal points". A negative number is a price increase. A positive is a price reduction. The formula for the first cell is written as:

$$=(J2-G2)/J2$$

Column S - Reviewer comments – this is where the person running the report will put comments on discrepancies that are discovered. Some comments will not need a response from the buyer, such as "Requoted" or "Revision Change". They just need to be noted for later use when the quarterly summary is created. For the comments that do need an explanation, such as "PO price doesn't match notes" or "No price in system", change the cell to pink after the note is written. This will flag the buyer to investigate. Put the date the note was entered.

Column T - Buyer comments – this is where the buyers will respond to the pink comments. They can ignore the ones that are not pink. Like you, they should be dating all their notes.

Column U – Resolution – this is the column the original reviewer uses to note if the situation was resolved or ask another question. If the situation is resolved, a note of "date - OK" is acceptable. At this point, the reviewer can change the pink cell to green. This will make the final review much easier and also make it easier for the buyers to see what is still open. NOTE: ALL notes in columns S, T, and U should have the date the note was entered.

Column V - Date PO Issued – this information will be input each day as the report is run.

**Processing the report**

The easiest way to process this report is in two separate steps.

Step 1 – Evaluate for allocations, lead times, and wrong parts being ordered. It will also help find parts that were ordered when there was already sufficient stock on hand. To do this, follow these instructions.

Add rows for any missing purchase orders. They may be missing because they were cancelled or the parts were received right away or if the buyer accidentally changed the purchase order entry date instead of the due date when issuing the purchase order.

Carry all formulas down to the last line of the spreadsheet.

Input the buyer information in Column I from the purchase order (if it isn't pulled in automatically) and put the date of the PO in column V.

In column L, highlight any value that is either "0.00" or above a predetermined amount. Let's use $200.00 for this exercise. The actual value will be determined by your company. Turn the numbers in the cell to red for better visibility. The object of this part of the process it to make sure the right parts are being ordered at the right time for the right usage.

Your spreadsheet should start looking like this:

Notice that the lines 2, 3 and 4 are not "0.00" or over $200.00 so they don't need to be investigated for this step.

Line 6 doesn't have a price in it, so it needs to be investigated. This one turned out to be a part that the supplier agreed to send a free sample but wanted a purchase order for tracking. Therefore, the note goes in the column N.

Lines 5, 7, 8 and 9 are over $200.00 so they will need to be investigated. Look up the allocations and enter them in column M.

Also, review if the quantity is correct for the allocations and safety stock. Do you need that many? Do you want to split the deliveries so you don't have more on hand than you need?

Does the due date listed bring the part in at the correct time? Will it be there when it is needed? Is it too early and needs to be stored? Is it within the listed lead time for that part? If the lead time is 80 days and it is needed in 30 days, did the buyer contact the supplier to make sure the date entered is reasonable?

If there is anything else that raises a flag or looks suspicious, investigate that as well and put the notes in column N. Turn the cell pink to signify that the buyer needs to respond.

After all parts are investigated, hide the columns you don't need for the next step. Your spreadsheet will look like this:

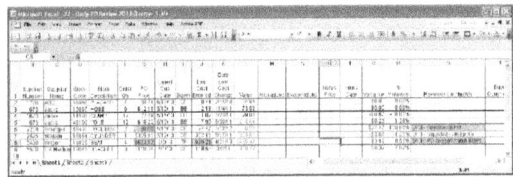

Step 2 – Evaluate for price increases. In order to do that, follow these instructions.

Evaluate any item in column Q that has a negative number larger than a predetermined amount. In this case we will use $2.00, since investigating small variances takes more time than the rewards warrant. Realistically, if you spend five minutes looking at a variance of $2.00 or less, you have lost money. The same goes for any quantity in column R that is less than 3%. A variance of $2.00 on a part that costs $2000.00 is such a small percentage; it is not worth spending time on. However, a variance of $2.00 on a part that costs $20.00 it is a big percentage. From a percentage aspect, 3% of $2000.00 is $60.00 but 3% of $20.00 is only $.60. Look at it this way; you will most likely buy significantly more of the $20.00 parts than you will the $2000.00, so the yearly impact is less on the higher priced part.

Lines 2 and 3 have no variation so they don't need to be investigated.

Lines 4 and 5 have a variation of less than $2.00 so they don't need to be investigated.

Line 6 is a positive number, but that is because the price on the purchase order is $0.00. You have already highlighted this issue for the buyer to address so you can ignore it.

Line 7 is a negative number so it needs to be investigated. Look up the part number and put the price from the notes in column O. Put the date of the notes in column P. In this case, let's say the part was requoted and this was the best price. Put the current date and "requoted" in column S. Since this is an acceptable reason for a cost increase, it doesn't need to be highlighted for further action.

Line 8 is also a negative number so it needs to be investigated. It shows in the notes that the price is $605.65 but the purchase order was written for $630.25. Put a note in column S with the current date and an explanation of the issue. This needs to be highlighted in pink for further follow up from the buyer.

Line 9 has a positive variance. In this case, look up the notes and make sure they match the purchase order, but you don't need to put notes in unless there is an issue.

Continue until all parts have been investigated.

The object of this part of the process is to make sure a price wasn't input incorrectly or that an increase wasn't accepted without doing everything possible to hold the price. This will also pick up parts that were ordered but shouldn't have been.

The acceptable categories for price increases are as follows:

1) Customer Specification or Single Source
2) Requoted (bought at best price)
3) Price more than 2 years old (but still needs to be requoted)
4) Revision Change
5) Higher Cost for Rush Order
6) Other (smaller quantity or other acceptable reason)

NOTE: "Price increase from supplier" is *always* an unacceptable reason for price increases. While they do happen, the buyer should requote or negotiate with the supplier to hold pricing.

Purchasing notes in your ERP system have a very real purpose. If you aren't using them, you should be. When buyers are first told to start using the notes section, they tend to think the objective is to fill up space. But the real objective is to transmit information. At first, the notes may be less useful than they should be, but as they get used to doing it, they will get better. Besides, if the notes don't have an acceptable reason for the increase, the reviewer will put notes in this report that the buyer has to address. After a few of those, they figure out that it is easier to put the information in correctly the first time.

Remember that the question the notes should answer is not "Why was there an increase?" but "What did you do to hold the cost?" There is a world of difference in those two questions. Once that difference is understood, the notes will get better.

If the notes say "Price increase from supplier" instead of something like "Requoted to………" or "negotiated single source", then the buyers are still answering the wrong question.

Also, if parts were requoted, all the requote information should be in the notes, Ie. Supplier, price, quote expiration date, lead time and any other relevant information for each supplier quoted.

Note that it is sometimes advisable to investigate *every* line item not just the ones that fall outside a certain range. This takes a considerable amount of extra time but may be worth it if want to make sure buyers are not just using "last cost" when they shouldn't be.

After the review is complete, save the shared file with the new date and notify the buyers that it is ready for their review. They will then investigate any items in pink. Before the next day's report is run, the reviewer has to look over the responses from the buyers (in column T) and make sure that the information is addressed and corrected. At this point the reviewer will put a note in column U that either says "Ok" or asks for further follow up. If the issue is addressed, the reviewer will change the pink cells to green. If there are more questions the cells will remain pink until all questions are answered. Remember to date all notes.

Each day you will run a new report and copy / paste the information into the existing spreadsheet, save with the new date and repeat the evaluation process.

The reason for running the report as a separate file first and then pasting it into your original report is that sometimes report writers overwrite any information already in a file. Better to do this in two steps than to wipe out all your hard work.

Just a caution here: What this report doesn't catch is if a price is entered on the PO and then changed at a later date. It is only a snapshot taken at the time the report is pulled.

## *Chapter 13 - Cost Containment Analysis*

At the end of each quarter, the Quarterly Analysis begins. Using the "Daily PO Review" spreadsheet, unhide all columns then save it one last time. Now "Save As" to "PO Analysis Quarter 1". Hide the columns that are not needed for this step. By now there should not be any remaining pink cells. Your new view should look like this:

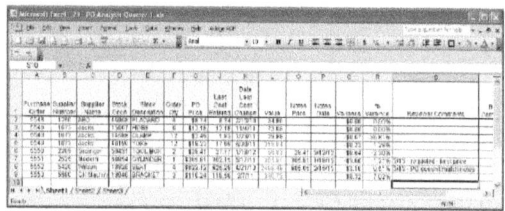

Insert two columns in front of column S. The first column will be labeled "Original Line Value" and the second one will be labeled "Reasons".

Now your spreadsheet will look like this:

Note that the values in column L – (Total Line Value) are based on the price entered in the purchase order times the quantity ordered. For column S – (Original Line Value), the information will be based on the original price (Last Cost Entered) times the quantity ordered. The formula for the first cell in column S is written as:

=J2*F2

Carry the formulas down to the last line that is populated.

Add a "sum" to the second blank line below the spreadsheet in columns in L and S.

Review the spreadsheet for any lines that have notes in column U. For every

131

note in column U, V and W, put a shortened note in column T with one of the "accepted" reasons listed. Note that all increases should be requoted or negotiated, but the "reason" listed is to explain why the requoting or negotiating couldn't be more effective.

All notes in column T should be one of the following:

> Customer specification / single source
> Requoted
> Old Price
> Rev Change
> Rush
> Other (This is for other <u>accepted</u> reasons. It is not a dumping ground for items that are hard to classify)

At the bottom of the spreadsheet, add the following information.

For this explanation, all formulas will be based on this spreadsheet. As explained before, each spreadsheet will have a different number of line items. Adjust the formulas as instructed in the section on Cost Reduction.

Enter the "Actual" spend in cell L16 by using a formula that is written as:

**=L11**

Enter the "Original" spend in cell L17 by using a formula that is written as:

**=S11**

Enter the "Difference" in cell L18 by using a formula that is written as:

**= L17-L16**

Enter the "% Difference" in cell L19 by using a formula that is written as:

**=L18/L17**

Enter the number of line items in cell B16. Notice that since the lines filled out are 2 through 9 and the first line is the header, that makes 8 lines of input.

Make sure you save the file at this point. It is a good idea to do a "Save As" and add a revision number to the file name.

Sort the list by column Q. Count how many line items are decreases, how many do not have a change and how many are increases. Enter those numbers in column B under "Summary". If you do a quick sum of the quantities in column B17 through B19, it should equal the value in cell B16.

Notice the items highlighted (L2 through L5) and notice the sum at the very bottom of the spreadsheet. It says "SUM=$607.41". This is the number you will want to put in cell D19.

Do the same for the "No change" and "Increases". Note that a "quick sum" on column D lines 17 through 19 should equal cell L11.

This is what your spreadsheet looks like now.

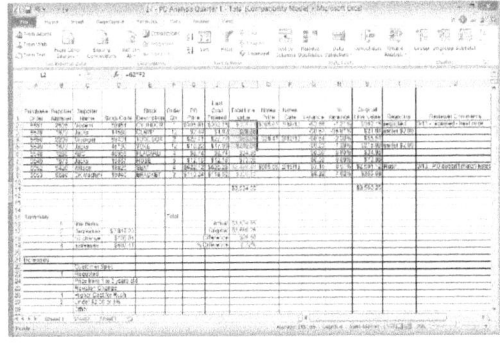

Next, sort your spreadsheet by column T. Enter the quantities for each line item under "Increases". The total of this column should equal the number in cell B19.

Repeat this process for cells D18 (no change) and D19 (increases). Your spreadsheet will look like this:

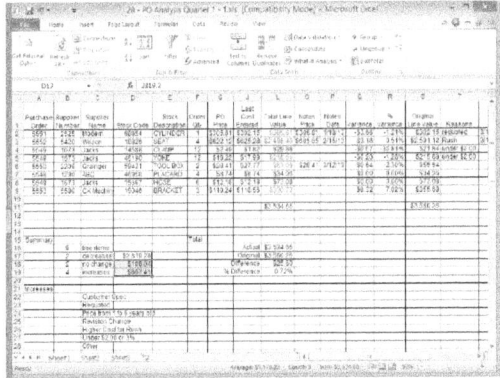

135

Note that a "quick sum" on column D lines 17 through 19 should equal cell L11.

The "decreases" and the "no change" items don't need any further investigation. The increases will be broken down by "reason".

To do this, resort the spreadsheet by column T. Count how many items fall into each category and enter them in cells D22 through D28.

Add a sum at the bottom of the "Increases" (cell B29). This number should match cell B19. It will look like this:

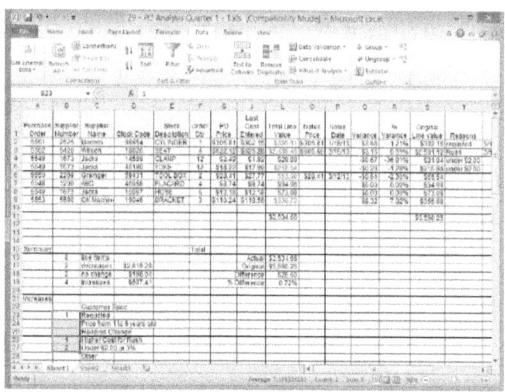

The last step in this process is to calculate what percentage of the totals is caused by each category. All cells

E17 through E28 should be formatted as Percent – "0" decimals

The formula for cell D16 is written as:

**=L16**

The formula for cell E17 is written as:

**=B17/B16**

The formula for cell E18 is written as:

**=B18/B16**

The formula for cell E19 is written as:

**=B19/B16**

The formula for cell E22 is written as:

**=B22/B19**

The formula for cell E23 is written as:

**=B23/B19**

The formula for cell E24 is written as:

**=B24/B19**

The formula for cell E25 is written as:

**=B25/B19**

The formula for cell E26 is written as:

**=B26/B19**

The formula for cell E27 is written as:

**=B27/B19**

The formula for cell E28 is written as:

**=B28/B19**

Because there are very few line items in this spreadsheet, it is not a true representation and you could calculate the percentages without the formulas. In a real project, that won't be as easy.

This is what your spreadsheet will look like now.

Note that the total of D17 through D19 should equal the sum in L11 and the sum of D22 through D28 should equal D19.

In a real cost containment project, there will be hundreds (more likely thousands) of lines. All of the values you will be inputting will be much higher and the sorting will be more extensive.

Since the number in L18 is positive, there was a cost decrease of $25.60 for the quarter. This creates a percentage increase of 0.72%. In real projects, your typical numbers will be in this range. In some cases, especially once the buyers start getting on board with the new process, there should be bigger decreases. Even if you have an overall increase, but it is smaller than 2%, you have probably done a very good job. Remember that overall increases in costs would normally average about 3%.

In an actual project, say that you spend two million dollars for the quarter. If you allowed the typical 3% increase, your increase would be $60,000.00. If you only hold it to 2% for the first quarter that you do this, your increase would be $40.000.00. That is a savings of $20,000.00 for the first quarter. So, if you manage to stay under the average increase, at least on the first couple quarters, consider it a successful project.

You may ask how this can be when you have done one or more cost reduction projects with perhaps an 8% to 10% savings. There are couple reasons for this. The cost reduction projects will take two to three months to complete. If you start the cost containment at the same time as the cost reduction, you won't see the results until the cost reduction is completed.

Also, keep in mind that a cost reduction is based on one machine or production line. It affects only a small portion of the entire purchases for the company. The balance of the parts being purchased are going to have to be dealt with as they come up for purchase. Even within a cost reduction project, there will be some parts that have price increases.

As you do more projects, the buyers will become more proactive with controlling costs and you will also be getting the "residual" savings.

Residual savings are the ones that don't get tracked anywhere, and, therefore, are somewhat invisible, but they are just as real. If your cost reduction shows you are buying five pieces of a part at a savings of $10.00 per piece, you will only show a savings of $50.00. In reality, if you use 100 of these parts per year, your savings is $500.00. This is still a savings, but it doesn't show up on any spreadsheets – except for the bottom line. _And, really, what other spreadsheet actually matters_?

Before you proceed to the PO Quarterly Summary Review, there is one more thing you can do with this report that could be very useful. If you want to see which supplier, commodity or buyer has the most or the largest increased or decreases, you can sort the spreadsheet by whichever value you choose. Do one last save and then save the file with a new name first so you don't risk losing any information. Next sort by the value you want to examine. Using the selected information, you can calculate percent of increase or decrease by dollar value, by supplier, or by buyer. You can evaluate it according to dollar value, percentages or by how many line items of each category.

If you saved the file to do the resorting and evaluating mentioned in the last paragraph, make sure you go back to the original file before you go to the next step.

**PO Quarterly Summary Review**

The final step is to track how you are doing from one quarter to the next. This is the way to see if your efforts are paying off. Whether you are doing a combination of cost reduction projects and the cost containment, or just the cost containment alone, you want to see if the numbers are improving. If they are improving, then your efforts are paying off. In some cases there may be other circumstances that affect the final numbers, such as the redesign of on entire machine. This may cause a "blip" on your spreadsheet, but can be taken into account.

Open a new Excel spreadsheet and name it "PO Quarterly Summary Review" and save in the appropriate folder.

Set it up to look like this:

Using the PO Analysis 1st Quarter spreadsheet that you have created, copy the appropriate information into the PO Quarterly Summary Review.

It will look something like this, but with much higher values. Note that the percentages calculated in column D in the spreadsheet above and column E in the spreadsheet below are calculated based on the number of purchase orders in each category, not the value of the purchase orders in each category.

If you want the percentages to be based on the value of the purchase order relative to the total amount spent, you can adjust the formulas by following this set of instructions.

Using the information in the "PO Analysis 1st Quarter" spreadsheet, follow the formulas below to obtain the spreadsheet shown here.

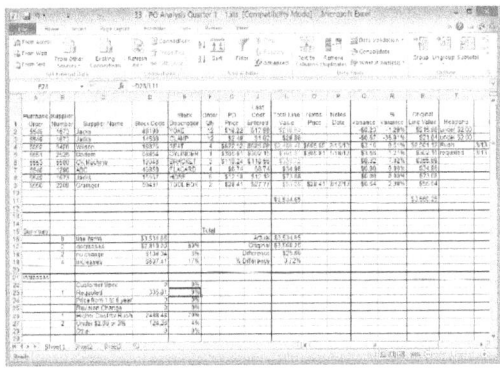

Cell E17 – the formula is:

**=D17/L11**

Cell E18 – the formula is:

**=D18/L11**

Cell E19 – the formula is:

**=D19/L11**

Cell E22 – the formula is:

**=D22/L11**

Cell E23 – the formula is:

**=D23/L11**

Cell E24 – the formula is:

**=D24/L11**

Cell E25 – the formula is:

**=D25/L11**

Cell E26 – the formula is:

**=D26/L11**

Cell E27 – the formula is:

**=D27/L11**

Cell E28 – the formula is:

**=D28/L11**

As you can see, you can select any number of values to compare simply by adjusting your formulas. It will all be determined by what information you want your report to reflect.

Each quarter, the new information will be input into the appropriate block of the spreadsheet.

At the end of the year, create a new tab for the next year and continue to fill out the information each quarter. As you get more quarters filled in, you will be able to track your progress.

It would be good to note here that once a cost is changed in your ERP system that is the number you will be using to compare your purchase order prices to. If a cost reduction project has been completed and the pricing changed, your totals on the cost containment project won't show up as an actual savings. However, the money has still been saved and will be accounted for in the Cost Reduction Project instead.

## *Chapter 14 – Summary*

With material costs rising every year you have to be proactive with your cost reduction and cost containment to stay competitive. Whether you do only one type of project or both types, you will still see the benefits. Even if you only do one cost reduction project per year instead of one per quarter, you will save money, but I truly believe that after the results of the first project are reviewed, you will want to do one every quarter.

It would be wonderful if every part you purchase could be requoted every time for the best price and lead time or if you could just tell your suppliers they need to reduce their cost by a certain percentage, but in the real world that isn't practical. It would even be nice if you could pass all your price increases on to your customers, but that isn't practical either. This approach gives you a tool that is not only practical, but also very effective in holding or even increasing your profit margin.

There has been a lot of "trial and error" in the development of this process. If you have ever set up a spreadsheet, started inputting information and then part way through realized you forgot a piece of data you should have been collecting and had to go back, you are probably sitting there nodding your head right now and saying, "Yup. Been there. Done that. Bought the shirt."

I have tried to remove most of the learning curve for you. Following the steps in this book should save you a lot of time, not to mention your sanity. You might even want to read the book twice, once for concept and once for detail, highlighting as you read. As with anything, the detail makes more sense once you understand the concept.

Choosing your resources is as important as choosing your target project. A great project can not have great results if the people doing it are unwilling or unable to grasp the concept and provide the necessary commitment and correct detail.

A typical project should take two to three months. Less than that doesn't give the person time to properly set up, evaluate, quote, chase quotes and enter details. Remember, your suppliers have other customers to service besides you. Any more time than that and people tend to lose focus.

If they have several months to do the project, they may put it off in favor of hotter issues and then have to rush at the end. If the project is over 1000 line items, you might be better off to break it down into two projects if possible, or take the lower dollar value parts out or maybe only do the longest lead time parts.

Depending on your company policy, there may be things you want to add or leave out. One company may allow the buyers to make cost changes and another may not. Keeping in mind that making a cost change on a part that has pieces in stock will skew the cost of the parts you already have.

I've tried to make the instructions specific enough so they have the detail needed for a successful project, but generic enough that any company can use them. I've also tried to point out the possible pitfalls to avoid frustration, lost time and a bad result.

The benefit of doing these projects is that you can see real, quantifiable (not to mention substantial) savings in as little as two to three months and they are relatively inexpensive to do – even if you do them externally.

There is probably no other single area in your entire company that you can see 300% to 400% return on investment. If you buy a new machine that is faster and more efficient, you probably wait months or even years for it to pay for itself and start actually _making_ you money. With these projects the savings happen as soon as the parts are purchased.

As you go through this book, you will see there are a lot of decisions to be made. I have tried to give you all the information you will need in order to make the right decisions for your company.

If your internal people have the skills and the time to do them, that may be a good choice for you. If not, a consultant may be a better option since you only pay them when they are needed for a project.

Although the main focus of these projects is cost reduction and cost containment, the other benefits are also very important.

- Shorter lead times make parts available when they are needed

and reduce the need for safety stock on some items.
- Smaller Economic Batch Quantities mean less parts to store, less money tied up in inventory and greater inventory turns.
- Pricing being held longer means less time spent verifying pricing or requoting parts as often.
- Reviewing high dollar purchases eliminates errors in delivery dates, pricing or just data entry.
- Reviewing all cost increases to see what was done to hold or reduce the costs determines if the cost increase was truly unavoidable.

Remember, the question is never "Why was there an increase?" The question is always "What did you do about it?"

### Note to Buyers:

Once management has reviewed the spreadsheets, you will undoubtedly be looking at doing more projects. How could they *not* be impressed by the savings? And now that you have done one project, the following projects will become easier. Did I also mention there is a certain thrill in seeing the final numbers and knowing *you did that!?*

You will no doubt find some shortcuts or favorite ways to do things. That is perfectly normal once you learn the process and can manage the spreadsheets. Management may want to see other results from your spreadsheets. And why not, there is a wealth of information hidden in these projects that can be pulled out by doing simple sorts. If you keep all your finished projects and quarterly reports in folders so you can find them, you may discover other uses for them based on what you might want to see.

**Note to Management:**

You really have nothing to lose by doing these projects. I can't guarantee you will save money, but *I will tell you that **every** Cost Reduction project we have ever done has saved more than it cost.*

Now that you have become proactive with cost reduction and cost containment, you can scrap the old catapult and spend your time polishing your new 155 Howitzer. Oh, and watching your profits grow!

If you are creative with ideas, you will find other ways this collected information can be of use. Once the work is done, don't hesitate to get all the use out of it that you can. You can find the top priced parts, the biggest savings, the best negotiations, the busiest buyer, the most proactive buyer, and even projected savings, just by sorting the information you already have gathered.

Now that you have an understanding of the process, order the full sized, full color workbook so your buyers can get started saving you money right away.

I started this book with a quote and I will end it with the same quote.

IF YOU ALWAYS DO WHAT YOU ALWAYS DID YOU WILL ALWAYS GET WHAT YOU ALWAYS GOT.

*If you would like to share your success stories or if you would like help with your Cost Reduction Projects or Cost Containment Projects, fell free to contact us. We can help you evaluate your situation, choose your projects, set them up, or even train your people to do it internally using our proven methods – whatever suits your needs.*

*Feel free to contact me at
Janice@entire360.com*

If this book has been helpful, please consider posting a review on Amazon. You can find it in books under the author – Janice Czaplewski.

*Left blank for personal notes*

## *Chapter 15 – Excel Hints*

**1) Sharing**

Sharing a file enables more than one person to work on a spreadsheet at the same time.

In your Excel spreadsheet, look at the top toolbar and find "Tools". Left click on "Tools" and you will see a drop down box. In the drop down box, click on "Share Workbook" and then a new screen will open. Click on the box next to "Allow changes by more than one user at the same time" then click "Ok". It may ask you if you want to save the file again. Click "yes". Now more than one person can use the spreadsheet. When one person saves the file, it will be visible to the other users. However, they won't be able to see it until they also hit "Save". If anyone is going to do a "Save As" on a shared file to rename it, all the other users must have saved their changes and closed the file first. If not, anyone with an open file will lose their changes. *Always* "Save" one last time before you do a "Save As" to capture all changes.

**2) Freeze Panes**

Freezing panes will keep the column headings visible to help ensure you are typing in the correct column.

In your Excel spreadsheet, highlight the first row below the headings by left clicking on number of that row on the far left side. On the main toolbar at the top, you will see "Window". Left click on "Window" and then click on "Freeze Panes". Now you can scroll down in your spreadsheet and still always have the column headings available.

### 3) Formulas

Formulas serve several purposes. They save having to manually enter results in the spreadsheet. Formulas will update if one of the "input" cells changes its value. They can be copied to another cell, and they will recalculate relative to the same position. In other words, if your formula in cell G6 is "=B6*F6" and you copy cell G6 and paste it into cell G7, it will recalculate as "=B7*F7". Notice that the column designation stays the same, but the row designation will change to match the new row you have pasted the cell into. With this, you can write one formula and copy it to all the cells in that column rather than calculate each cell individually. Formulas will quickly become your new "best friend".

In your Excel spreadsheet, click on the cell where you want your formula to be. Formulas generally start with the equal sign "=".

To add the values in only two cells, type "=", then type in the column and row designation of the first cell. Note that the column designation is always before the row designation. Next type "+" and then the column and row designation of the second cell. Hit "Enter" and your formula is complete.

Another option is to type "=", click on the cell you want to add, click on "+" and then click on the second cell you want to add. Finish your formula by hitting "Enter".

To add the values in more than two cells *in the same column*, type "=" and then "SUM" in the cell where you want your formula to appear. Now you will want to type "(", then click on the first cell in the column. Now type ":" and click on the last cell in the column and then close the formula with ")". Note that you do not type in the quotation marks. Hit "Enter" and your formula will be complete.

Your other option is to highlight all the cells in the column and continue highlighting until you reach a blank cell.

While those cells are highlighted, click on the "sum" symbol on the top toolbar. It looks like this: $\Sigma$

If you just need to see a result, but don't necessarily need it to show up in the spreadsheet, you can do a "quick sum". This is useful if you just want to do a "logic" check on your numbers. To do a "quick sum" simply highlight the cells you want to view and see the sum appear at the bottom of your spreadsheet in the border. Note that <u>all</u> the values in the highlighted area will be added.

To subtract, multiply or divide, use the same steps but substitute "-" to subtract, "*" to multiply or "/" to divide.

For formulas in this book, type them exactly as they appear unless instructed otherwise. If you add spaces or miss a parentheses the formula won't work.

Also, it is worth noting that nothing is nothing but "0" is something. If you put a "0" in a cell to designate a no quote instead of "NQ" and are using the formulas to calculate the lowest cost, the formula will see the "0" and choose that as the lowest cost. If you leave the cell blank (nothing) the formula won't pick it up but you may forget that they responded with a "no quote" and you will waste time (not to mention being embarrassed) chasing quotes you have already received. If you put "NQ" it the cell, you can remember that you are done with it and not risk picking up the "0" in your formula.

**4) Hide and unhide**

Your spreadsheet is going to get very big very fast. Hiding and unhiding columns or rows is a very useful function in this kind of spreadsheet. If you can get columns (or rows) out of your way when you are not using them, the spreadsheet will fit on your screen better and look less complicated, making it easier to find the cell you are trying to put information into. I would caution you to "Hide" not "Delete" or "Move" the information you aren't using. If you accidentally "Delete" the information and then hit "Save" it is gone forever!!! Recreating the information from the last saved spreadsheet will take a very long time and probably cause you to use more colorful words than you have ever used before.

In your Excel spreadsheet, highlight the column you want to hide by left clicking on the column designation at the top. Then right click anywhere in the highlighted area. A pop up box will appear. In the box, click on "Hide". In order to "Unhide" the column when you need it, highlight the column on either side of the one you want to see. Then right click anywhere in the highlighted area. In the pop up box that appears, click on "Unhide".

**5) Sorting**

If formulas are your new best friend, sorting will become your new "Second Best" Friend. During the course of this project you will sort and resort the information several times. At various points you will want to sort by supplier, part number, description or other values.

In your excel spreadsheet, highlight all the rows you want to sort by left clicking on the row designation on the left for the first row you want to include. Drag the mouse to the row designation for the last row you want to include. Once they are highlighted, left click on "Data" on the top tool bar. When you see the drop down box, click on "Sort". Another box will open. Use the first drop down arrow to select the column you want to sort by and whether you want it ascending or descending. Then click "Ok".

**6) Multiple Sorts**

This is useful if you want to do a sort within a sort. If, for example, you want to sort all the parts from one supplier by the part number you would use this. Follow the instructions above, highlighting all the rows. Then in your sort, you would choose "supplier" in the top box and "Part Number" in the second box. Or if you want to find all the "Cylinders" and who supplies them, sort first by "Description" and then by "Supplier". If all your part descriptions follow the same format, such as "Bearing, Browning 3", it is a lot easier because all bearings or cylinders or hoses or whatever will show up in the same sort. If you use a different format, you may have to dig a little deeper or do more than one sort to get the information you want.

**7) Set up folders**

Putting files in folders and subfolders is an excellent way to keep information organized and easy to find.

Whether you are setting up folders in email or on your computer, the process is the same. Highlight the folder you want to build your new folders in. On the top of the screen you have open, click on "File", then "Folder" then "New Folder". A new folder will appear with the name "New Folder". You can then rename the folder to suit your needs. You can then add sub folders by clicking on the new folder you just renamed and following the steps above. Note that if at any point you want to change the name of a folder, simply right click on the folder name and select "Rename" from the box that appears.

**8) Attach Files**

To attach a drawing to an email, find the appropriate file and select the appropriate drawings by holding down the "control" key while clicking on the numbers. Right click on the highlighted drawings and select "Copy". Go to a blank space on the email and right click again. Select "Paste". This will put the drawings into the "attachment" area of the email. Send the email.

OR

To attach a drawing to an email, click on "Desktop". Then click on "New Folder". Go to the desktop folder "Drawings" and select the appropriate drawings by holding down the "control" key while clicking on the numbers. Right click on the highlighted drawings and select "copy". Go to a blank space on the body of your email and right click again. Select paste. This will put the drawings into the "attachment" area of the email. Send the email.

**9) Zip Files**

When a file is too large to email, it is helpful to compress or "zip" the file first.

To zip a file, find the appropriate folder and right click on it. Select "Send To" and then "Compressed (zipped) folder". The new "zipped" file will appear at the bottom of the original folder. Note that the icon with the file now shows a zipper. The original file will remain as it was. Right click on the zipped file and select "Copy" to copy to an email or FTP folder. Right click on the desired location and select "paste"

**10) Format cells**

Formatting changes how the information in a cell is displayed, whether it is a number, a date, a percentage or some other value.

In your Excel spreadsheet, right click on the cell, column or row you want to format. You will see a drop down box appear. Left click on "format cells". Another screen will open. In the "Category" column, click on the appropriate category and you will see the "Type" column change to the choices for that category. Categories like Number, Currency and Accounting will give you additional options such as the number of places after the decimal point, using a comma to separate numbers, or using a dollar sign. Click on the appropriate choices and then click "Ok".

**11) Find**

When you have a very large spreadsheet it would be nearly impossible to locate an individual number or word. "Find" will help you do this quickly.

In your spreadsheet, make sure you only have one cell highlighted. If you have more than one cell highlighted, the "Find" will only search the highlighted cells. On the top tool bar, click on "Edit". This will open the drop down box. Choose "Find". It will open another box. In the "Find What" box, type in the number or word you want found. Click "Find Next" and the first time that word or number appears will be highlighted. You can then review or change the cell or click "Find Next" again to find the next appearance of that number or word.

Again, in Excel there is usually more than one way to get the results you want. It will also depend on what version of Excel you are using. This only gives you one way.

*If you would like to share your success stories or if you would like help with your Cost Reduction Projects or Cost Containment Projects, fell free to contact us. We can help you evaluate your situation, choose your projects, set them up, or even train your people to do it internally using our proven methods – whatever suits your needs.*

*janice@entire360.com.com*

If this book has been helpful, please consider posting a review on Amazon. You can find it in books under the author – Janice Czaplewski.

www.ingramcontent.com/pod-product-compliance
Lightning Source LLC
Chambersburg PA
CBHW051701170526
45167CB00002B/489